"USED TO BE A ROUGH PLACE IN THEM HILLS"

MOONSHINE, THE DARK CORNER, AND THE NEW SOUTH

Joshua Beau Blackwell

authorHOUSE®

AuthorHouse™
1663 Liberty Drive, Suite 200
Bloomington, IN 47403
www.authorhouse.com
Phone: 1-800-839-8640

This book is a work of non-fiction. Unless otherwise noted, the author and the publisher make no explicit guarantees as to the accuracy of the information contained in this book and in some cases, names of people and places have been altered to protect their privacy.

First published by AuthorHouse   1/19/2009

ISBN: 978-1-4389-3470-9 (sc)

Library of Congress Control Number: 2008912102

Printed in the United States of America
Bloomington, Indiana

This book is printed on acid-free paper.

To Oscar Blackwell:

A man who chose to take the hard step to feed his family by any means necessary.

Preface

The foundations for this book originated in the thesis I submitted for my Masters of History at the University of Charleston. The study tackled the issue of New South development within Greenville County, South Carolina and the subsequent oppression of pre-modern cultures that continued to cling to their own existence. After the success of the thesis and the continued loss of Dark Corner wilderness due to gated-community development, I felt that the following was a story that should be told.

Unchecked development and modernization has been a bane for South Carolina culture since the 1970s. The continual gentrification of impoverished cultures for the benefit of the upper-class is a shameful trend that knows no bounds. Whether it is the loss of traditional Gullah lands in the Lowcountry, the "whitening" of the Charleston Peninsula, the extinction of Appalachian culture within the State, or the simple loss of ones southern accent for a bland and clean pronunciation; the cultural wealth of South Carolina has greatly suffered in recent memory.

As a young child, I was exposed to a culture that was in its death throws. My great-grandfather was a moonshiner seasonally, and my father used to regale me with stories of his experiences. Knowing full well what went on in the remote sections of Hogback Mountain, I was always drawn to it as a child. Many times throughout the winter months, my father and I would spend whole weekends on the summit of the mountain; amongst the ruins of an old hunting lodge that was a moderate hike from the now defunct South Carolina Highway 118.

The following work is partly a reflection of my regret of the loss of a world long since past. This is my attempt to both eulogize and explain a cultural phenomenon, while overlooked and persecuted, that ranked among the most colorful of American cultures. While an extremely personal topic to undertake, I have made a conscious effort to distance myself enough to give the topic a fair and analytical treatment.

There are many who deserve thanks for the inspiration and execution of this work. My father is owed a special debt of gratitude for introducing me to the history of the Dark Corner at an early age. I consider myself a very fortunate man for having inherited his love of the Dark Corner and the wilds of Appalachian South Carolina. My mother managed to instill in me her calm collectiveness that has enabled me to keep focused all of these years, without which none of this could have been possible.

My Grandparents inspired me through their desire to keep the family ties taut with their heritage, which served as the corner stone for this entire work. Next, Barney Barnwell, and other more colorful individuals that I have met in the moonshine community of Appalachian South Carolina, are owed much thanks for providing a more personal insight into the subject. Also, I would like to extend a special thanks to Rebecca Saunders for providing some of the illustrations for this work. Furthermore, David Gleeson, W. Scott Poole, and Bo Moore are owed a great debt of gratitude for their efforts and patience in assisting my treatment of this topic at the University of Charleston. Finally, this work could not have been possible without the long hours of editing and arguing, without recompense, that my best friend Sarah Caldwell endured in providing the forced labor necessary to produce anything worth publishing.

Hendersonville, South Carolina
October 2008

Contents

Introduction

Appalachian South Carolina

On a warm summer Sunday in 1891, parishioners of Greenville County's Mountain Hill Church began to arrive from the small farms that dotted the coves of Hogback and Glassy Mountain. It was the twenty-third of August and the church, an old log and stone structure, had been opened earlier that morning to circulate air throughout the sanctuary. As many were standing around talking about the week's events that ranged from the progress of the corn crop to weather, Richard Gosnell traversed the churchyard. In route from his buggy with a bottle of wine for the communion service, Gosnell passed the Howard clan. Reputedly, the Howards and the Gosnells had no love lost for one another, and each family kept their eyes open for an opportune time to insult the other.[1]

As Gosnell walked passed the Howards, Joshua Howard called out to Richard, "do you mean to slight me and mean that as an insult?" Ignoring the bait, Gosnell continued towards the sanctuary. As Gosnell prepared to enter the church, James Howard produced a revolver and shot at him. The bullet, missing Gosnell, lodged in the exterior wall of the church. What followed was a melee that has been engrained in the folklore of the South Carolina mountains ever since.[2]

The shot fired by Howard was the inaugural action in a general row that had been building for sometime. Richard Gosnell's daughter had been recently beaten in the church yard by Babe Durham, the employer of Joshua Howard. Luther Durham, another member of the clan, was working as a magistrate and had a warrant in his possession for James Howard. According to the warrant, authorities wanted him for the disruption of a congregational meeting at the very same church a few weeks earlier.

As the first shots rang out, many of the male parishioners sprang for cover and produced firearms of their own. In the skirmish that followed, the Howards were supported by members of the congregation with whom they had family ties. The majority of parishioners who witnessed the aggression reacted in self-defense. The Durhams, seeing an opportune time to settle old scores, began to fire in a multitude of directions. Although the Howards initiated the conflict, the result was not to their advantage.[3]

After the smoke cleared, it was obvious that the Howards had taken the brunt of the fight. In a fire-fight that saw upwards of fifty rounds exchanged, several parishioners lay wounded in the churchyard. Joshua Howard had been pierced by a ball, which had entered his back, and he would die early Monday afternoon. His brother Tim had taken a non-fatal round to the head, while Dick Howard had been shot in the arm. Luther Durham had fared no better than the other participants after being gut shot, while also catching a ball directly in the mouth severing his tongue. To round out the carnage a supporter of the Gosnell's, Sherman Bridgeman, had been slightly wounded with a grazing shot to the head. [4]

All interviewed following the fight noted that the incident was a direct result of an altercation between the Howards and the Gosnells on the previous Saturday evening. Most of the participants, still drinking as of Sunday morning, had arrived at the church to settle the affair. Little was done in the way of law enforcement. As the sheriff attempted to make an inquest into the event, he was welcomed at the border of the community by an armed posse and persuaded to turn back towards his office in Greenville.[5]

This particular anecdote is indicative of a phenomenon that once occurred frequently in northwestern South Carolina. As South Carolina emerged as a pillar of antebellum Southern culture; another community, almost the polar opposite of the dominant ideology of the Palmetto State, was nestled in an isolated region of the State.[6] While the majority of South Carolina developed a deep market economy that hinged on the cultivation of cotton through chattel slavery and a paternalist society that became unified from the coast to the foothills, one small segment of the State's population took a direction that differed from their fellow Carolinians.[7] This collection of people could be found nestled in a far removed corner of the State; the "Dark Corner."

While geographically identified with South Carolina, the Dark Corner was a separate cultural area that presented clear contrast from the cultures predominate in the rest of the State. While much of the State unified as a cohesive political and economic entity, the Dark Corner retained many of its unique cultural qualities. One such quality of significant importance was the area's dependency on home distillation and the widespread violence that resulted from the practice. Nestled along the Blue Ridge Mountains, the Dark Corner maintained closer ties to Appalachian culture, than the cultural influences predominant in the rest of South Carolina. The end result was that the Dark Corner became largely disconnected to the antebellum cotton economy, the secession movement, and, most importantly, the modernization of the New South following the American Civil War.[8]

The story of the Dark Corner is one of isolation, misleadingly simple culture, conflict, and violence. This work will begin by examining the Dark Corner's history and the economic differences that developed separating it from the remainder of the Palmetto State. Second, the troubles of the Dark Corner and its tradition of lawlessness will be examined in a case study of the resistance to Federal authority following the establishment of the Excise Taxes on alcohol in 1866. Next, the cultural differences of the Dark Corner will be surveyed through the writings of contemporary New South editors and their perceptions the "rustics" of the mountain regions of South Carolina. Finally, the oral tradition of the Dark Corner will be examined to see what the consensus of its legacy is, what qualities of the Appalachian culture remain, and in particular, what its attitude towards illicit liquor has been.

For a clear understanding of the Dark Corner's cultural separation from much of South Carolina, it is necessary to briefly explain the parameters of Appalachian culture.[9] No other cultural identity can be more comfortably associated with the inhabitants of the Dark Corner than that of Appalachian culture. Dark Corner economy, mannerisms, and methods of interaction reflected the traits common to Appalachia more than the culture of the rest of South Carolina. Five clear traits of Appalachia were present in the Dark Corner: a permanent yeoman economy, fewer restrictions on a woman's role in society, unique speech patterns, culturally accepted violence often linked to illicit alcohol, and the blood feud.

It is generally acceptable to paint a picture of Appalachia as a society that was self-sufficient to some extent; particularly following the colonial period. Appalachian society was a yeoman stylized culture that was economically dependent upon patch farming and plateau grazing. This society, spanning through miles of ridges and hollows, provided the United States' its last functional yeoman economy in which trade and communication were tied together through its small villages and churches.[10]

This cultural trait was well developed and wide spread throughout Appalachia by the start of the nineteenth century and was only interrupted by the Civil War. While most other regions in the United States witnessed yeoman farming as a stage on the way to larger commercial farming; the yeoman culture that developed in the Southern Appalachians was not a stage; it was the norm.[11] The yeoman economies present in the Appalachian South prior to the Civil War were a far cry from the plantation economies common to the lowland and piedmont South. The Dark Corner of South Carolina exercised a yeoman style economy throughout all of the nineteenth century.[12] This cultural anomaly distinguished the Dark Corner and Southern Appalachia from much of the South during many of the key political struggles that dominated the period.[13]

Southern Appalachia's view of domestic roles also differed from the lowland South. The virtue of womanhood and the role of male dominance centered less on a society-wide need to preserve the status-quo than it did on the immediate preservation of the family or clan. In relationships, yeoman women had been traditionally viewed as working minor-partners instead of subservient icons of virtue that needed to be protected from society's ills.[14] This interpretation of the role of women is evident in the liquor production of the Dark Corner. In many instances, the main participants in crimes or in family distillation operations were women. In fact, women occasionally went as far as to spring their husbands from jail after being arrested for liquor violations and related crimes.[15]

Another element of Appalachian culture is its distinct take on the English language and the noticeable dialectic differences from

American English. It has been argued that the distinctive nature of Appalachian speech was a result of the heavy Scots-Irish settlement into the region.[16] Many language enthusiast believe that the use of strong past-tense verb forms, irregular verbs, old fashion prepositions, early English participles, and a heavy stress on final syllables created a speech pattern and dialect that is metered similar to that of nursery rhymes and ballads. This metered language and the distortion of verbs is unique to Appalachia; a syntax component that separates it from other dialects of the English language.[17]

Appalachian speech is a modern connection to the speech patterns and syntax of the colonial settlers of the Southeast.[18] The use of –e and –in as opposed to –ing at the end of verbs, and a heavy reliance on the prefix a– are vestiges of the early Scots-Irish and English settlement of the region. Coupled with this syntax is a working use of metaphors, similes, omissions of sounds, reduction of syllables in words, and colloquialisms that provides Appalachian speech with a creative breadth not seen in many other dialects. [19]

In the Dark Corner of South Carolina these syntax traits are present, particularly amongst the elderly population. Their dialectic differences have been noted by many who have shown interest in the region. As late as 1980, the distinctive Appalachian syntax was recorded in the isolated pockets of the Dark Corner. In an interview with two of the elderly female residents of Glassy Mountain Township; a reporter inquired of Luemer and Della Plumley about the introduction of electricity into their portion of the Dark Corner. Frustrated with the failure of Duke Power to live up to the promise to send a lineman out to the coves to introduce electricity, Leumer Plumley quipped that:

Deller, I just as well cook us some dinner. We're not a-going git no power today." "Well Dooty," said Della,

**"is that what you wuz a-wating fer?" "Been a-lookin'
to git it up here fer 25 years and it didn't come," she
said, "Just till we got so old we can't enjoy it."[20]**

One of the earliest to actively study the topic of Appalachian
culture, John C. Campbell, once claimed that the dominant trait of
the Southern Appalachian was "independence raised to the fourth
power."[21] This independent streak was certainly an attribute that
separated the Dark Corner from the remainder of South Carolina.
However, this streak had an unfortunate side; the common use of
extreme violence. Campbell broke down homicide rates at the turn
of the twentieth century and found that the Appalachian Mountains
were per capita, one of the most violent places in the United States.[22]

The Dark Corner of South Carolina provides lots of quintessential
examples of how violence was intertwined with Appalachian
culture. Lawlessness and violence had always been a fixture in the
Dark Corner. The 1797 murder of Greenville County's first sheriff,
while patrolling the Dark Corner, was a foreboding sign of later
developments.[23] During the latter portions of the nineteenth century,
as well as in the early twentieth century, lawlessness was common in
many coves of the Dark Corner.

The community adopted violent means as their own form of
conflict resolution. Dark Corner violence was at such a level by the
late nineteenth century that local newspaper outlets were openly
calling on state authorities in Columbia to put a stop to it. As the
editor of the Greenville based *Enterprise and Mountaineer* put it: "The
wildest part of the West could exhibit no more wanton disregard of
law and order."[24]

One violent measure that was prominent in the Dark Corner,
but relatively unseen in other areas of the State, was the blood feud.[25]
The independent nature of Appalachian residents, the isolation of

the culture, and the major emphasis on the ties of one's family set the stage for the birth and the continuation of many generational feuds. The folk interpretation of Appalachia holds that the feud tradition is a remnant from the colonial settlement of the Scots-Irish and the English. However, the blood feud and inter-personal violence can also be viewed as a supplemental quasi-law in areas where the court system was weak or nonexistent. This was usually a manifestation of what the offended perceived as right and within the moral order.[26]

The bloodshed and unrest that was common in the Dark Corner was certainly an example of these Appalachian traits. Dean Crain, a Dark Corner native who wrote a narrative about his boyhood in the 1890s, remembered the depth of the feud within the Dark Corner. He recalled that the violent expectations for being crossed were so intense that, "there was scarcely a boy in the neighborhood above twelve years old who did not carry a pistol."[27] These boys were armed with the express intention of extracting some form of retribution from those that they had been brought up to resent or to swiftly address any personal insults brought down on them by others. While South Carolina was known for having an especially violent culture, the use of extreme violence lasted longer in the Dark Corner than in other portions of the State.[28]

With these components of Appalachian culture the Dark Corner had the distinction of being in South Carolina, but not being truly part of the State. When the State began to solidify politically during the antebellum period, the Dark Corner would stand alone as a remote community fraught with the backwardness of unionism.[29] During the Civil War, the Dark Corner hosted deserters from two states, and proved such a thorn in the side of conscript officers that it was largely abandoned as a place for Confederate recruitment.[30] When industrialization came to South Carolina in a large way after the Civil War, the New South boosters targeted the Dark Corner as the complete opposite of what good South Carolinians should be.[31] Finally, much of the region's trouble with State and Federal authorities, following changes in liquor laws, can be ultimately related to the independent and economic qualities of Appalachian culture found in the Dark Corner.[32] For those residing in modernized Greenville at the turn of the twentieth century, the Dark Corner truly was home to another culture locked in another time, but it was actually just an outpost of strong Appalachian culture in the Palmetto State.[33]

Chapter One

The "Dark Corner"

The Geographic Conundrum

The location of the Dark Corner is almost as ambiguous as the region is notorious. This cultural enclave that witnessed so many violent crimes and served as a haven for illicit distillation has eluded definitive boundaries despite its reputation. Various writers and historians throughout the years have sought to nail down the exact location of the Dark Corner. Naturally, many of these attempts differ in their conclusions about the geographic boundaries of the area. However, given the abundance of accounts and similarity amongst them, a common consensus can be inferred.

Local newspaperman and amateur historian James Walton Lawrence, Sr. has argued that the Dark Corner can be pinpointed to the small township of Glassy Mountain, which occupies the northeastern most corner of Greenville County.[34] On the other hand historian Mann Batson expands the boundaries presented by Lawrence to include the township directly south of Glassy Mountain, Highlands.[35] However, with cultural practices common to the Dark Corner found in other portions of the mountains of South Carolina; one can successfully argue that the boundaries of the Dark Corner include the extremes of northwestern Spartanburg County and parts of Western North Carolina. For the purpose of this study, the Dark Corner of South Carolina is defined as the northern rim of Greenville

County, the northwestern extremes of Spartanburg County, and the remote terrain of northeastern Pickens County. Four townships in particular have staked a claim in the Dark Corner of Greenville County. Cleveland, Glassy Mountain, Highland, and Saluda Townships have all witnessed events that gave the Dark Corner a notorious reputation for illegal activity in South Carolina.

While Cleveland, Highlands, and Saluda were isolated and could claim their fair share of illicit distillation, the epicenter for the illicit activity was Glassy Mountain Township. The township, center of the Dark Corner, bordered Greenville County's Gowansville and was in close proximity to the northwestern Spartanburg County towns of Landrum and Campobello. This community had the benefit of residing in a location where supplies were easily accessible from these railroad communities in the latter portions of the nineteenth century. Glassy Mountain Township's relative location to northwestern Spartanburg County, its isolation from the remainder of Greenville, and its border with North Carolina created a gray area for the community where questions over jurisdiction made law enforcement precarious.[36] This situation ultimately led to the creation of a safe haven for illicit activity. On occasions, however, liquor related violence would spread outside the Dark Corner.

Violence was witnessed in Landrum, as well as other northwestern Spartanburg County communities. Borderland distillers, most notably Lewis Redmond of Western North Carolina, sought refuge in the Dark Corner. Pickens County witnessed an almost identical flare up in post-Civil War violence as did the Dark Corner, and these two hotspots shared common participants.[37] Furthermore, the lower classes of the City of Greenville were the recipients of much of the illicit whiskey produced in the Dark Corner.[38] This angered the local boosters who turned their wrath on the people and the culture of the Dark Corner, who supplied a large volume of the town's alcohol. Likewise, the socially-conscious residents of the same city expended much of their energy in the suppression of the activities found throughout the mountains.

In his work, *The Upper Part of Greenville South Carolina*, Mann Batson agrees with the consensus that the Dark Corner's cultural hearth was within the northeastern portions of Greenville County, along the border of Spartanburg County and North Carolina. Aware of the social stigma that was attached with the area, Mann notes that for generations, locals who were asked by travelers as if they were in the Dark Corner were usually met with the response that, "it was just down the road."[39] Thus, not admitting to the exact location of the region by its inhabitants led to some confusion about the true boundaries of the Dark Corner.

Despite the debate of the exact location of the Dark Corner, the culture of independence, lawlessness, and distillation that developed there prior to the Civil War was brought to national attention in the late-nineteenth century as the area exploded with violence and disorder. The wilds of Greenville and Spartanburg counties were quickly heralded as a dangerous and lawless domain that shunned the laws of the United States, as observers became enthralled by accounts of the illicit activities of the Dark Corner.[40] Very quickly, cultural conflicts and changes in the legal codes of the country created a crucible of violence.[41] The situation that developed in the Dark Corner was outlined in countless contemporary articles and accounts.

The notion of a "Dark Corner," a location where laws, modernization, and morals are absent, is indeed an intriguing idea. However, where does such a nomenclature originate? In short, no one is exactly sure. The origins of the term "Dark Corner," in reference to the northern rim of Greenville County, are perhaps lost to history.

However, there are some traditional stories explaining the roots of this ominous term.

Former unionist governor Benjamin F. Perry noted that the origins of the name "Dark Corner" came from the region's resistance to the Nullification movement in the 1830s.[42] According to Perry, the Nullification movement hit a dead end in the mountains of Greenville County. When other portions of the Palmetto State endorsed Nullification whole heartedly, the residents of the upper four townships of Greenville County were decidedly against it. Perry recalled that the radical political elements from the lower elevations of the State proclaimed the Appalachian community, "the 'Dark Corner' of Greenville, a corner in which the light of Nullification could not shine."[43] History would show that the same went for the Secession vote as Perry continued, "Would the whole South had been such a 'Dark Corner' in 1861! It would have spared the lives of many hundreds of thousands of gallant, brave men, North and South." [44]

Others attribute the origin of the name to a speech given during the secession movement. According to tradition, a visiting politician was standing upon a wagon bellowing secessionist rhetoric to a less than receptive crowd. Growing weary of his argument and his company, a few local men removed the blocks from behind the wheels of the wagon and sent it rolling down the hillside into a thicket. Distraught from this ill reception in the mountains, the man was noted as saying that those in the hills were "in the Dark".[45]

Others attribute the birth of the term to less than colorful origins. Dean Crain, a early twentieth century novelist that grew up in the community, noted that the term Dark Corner originated with the region's notable violent past and the actions of men ruled by sin.[46] However, the term was certainly in common usage by the 1840s as the *Greenville Mountaineer* made note that an 1849 Fourth of July celebration in the "Dark Corner" was uneventful.[47]

The Dark Corner's origins, like much of the South Carolina upcountry, were different from those of the Lowcountry. In the upland regions of the Carolinas, settlement was primarily fueled by a southerly migration flowing out of the backwoods of Virginia and Pennsylvania after these areas began to fill with people, and not a westward migration funneling out of the Lowcountry. The result of this migration was the Carolina Appalachians being populated with inhabitants who had very little affiliation with their coastal-based governments.[48]

It was during the mid-eighteenth century that the first whites ventured into what later became known as the Dark Corner. James Walton Lawrence, Sr. claimed that the first white settlement in the area began around 1761 with a small trading fort along Vaughn Creek on the modern-day border of Greenville County, South Carolina and Polk County, North Carolina. The compound, which was built first as a trading post by illegal Indian traders, was later revamped into a fortified blockhouse. The location of the establishment was paramount, as this unidentified settlement overlooked an old Indian trail that was said to have stretched from coastal areas of South Carolina well into the Ohio River Valley.[49]

The bloody Cherokee War of 1760-61 put into motion a series of events that would ultimately encourage settlement in the area. In spite of the negative aspects of almost total isolation and the exaggerated image of rampant bands of "blood thirsty heathens" roaming the hillsides, the white population of the region grew as ambitious families pushed into the disputed lands between North and South Carolina. Understanding, however, that the threat from the Cherokee was real, local merchants took it upon themselves to ensure a greater security for themselves and their clientele. The new wave of migration into the region that occurred in the years following the War was widely the product of a series of blockhouses that were constructed at the various trading posts that were scattered throughout the region.[50]

Following the War, and the defeat of the Cherokee, and the resulting increase in the white population of the region, a boundary dispute between North and South Carolina developed. With the Cherokee threat in the immediate area shrinking, the question of colonial authority was raised as both North and South Carolina were providing settlement grants in the region. A 1772 survey and boundary readjustment placed the region that became the Dark Corner under the jurisdiction of South Carolina law. As with the culture that was developed by the original settlers' descendents, the founding communities of the late 1700s along Vaughn Creek and at Fort Gowan were operating in the convenient narrow flux that is afforded those who live along the fringes of established and enforceable law.

After the formal acceptance of the New Acquisition lands, surrendered by the Cherokee Indians to both North and South Carolina, State officials encouraged increased settlement in the hills of the backcountry.[51] By the late-eighteenth century, the Dark Corner had already begun to develop its liquor economy. As early as 1792, the inhabitants of the area were noted as distillers that "retail spirituous liquors to the malicious lots of the country and greatly encourage vice and immorality."[52]

Darkness Defined

By 1849 the citizens of Greenville were referring to the northern extremes of the county as the Dark Corner and were viewing it as something different from their portion of the county. A Greenville Newspaper remarked on the Dark Corner's sobriety in 1849:

> **Some three or four hundred of the citizens of the Dark Corner of Greenville, met at Old Bladensburg to celebrate the 4th of July, which was done in a very patriotic style… The whole was conducted with that unprecedented unanimity of sentiment, and a sobriety which sheds a luster on that part of the district.**[53]

The fact that the imagery of sobriety and unanimity warranted mention in a trivial account of the Dark Corner's Fourth of July celebration is indeed telling. Even as early as 1849, the rough nature of the inhabitants was well known locally. With fore knowledge of the stigma that the community had developed, the notion of Dark Corner citizens participating in an activity sober and not threatening each others existence was marketable news for the city of Greenville. It is clear that the Dark Corner was viewed as a festering thorn in the progressive image of Greenville County, when the author of the article concluded that the Dark Corner was indeed capable of "acting" the part of a citizen of Greenville.

During the Secession crisis and the opening months of the Civil War, the term "Dark Corner" evolved into a negative connotation synonymous with those who were unpatriotic.[54] The area's lack of support for secession and their general refusal to serve in the Confederate Army were a source of contempt for some Confederates.[55] One secessionist editor noted that, "Few Dark Corner men … have volunteered. It is to be hoped that some light will yet break upon their darkness."[56] While somewhat defined as a different place by the time of the Civil War, it was after the War when the Dark Corner earned its reputation as a unique area of South Carolina.

This distinction was earned by its response to regulation of the home distillation economy.

In spite of the evolution of the implications of the term "Dark Corner," one notable aspect of the Dark Corner remained constant. It, throughout much its history, had existed outside the normal parameters of organized law. The tradition of lawlessness had its roots in the American Revolution, when supporters of both sides exploited the area as both a refuge and an isolated target. Aside from residing in an area openly contested by the warring factions, the Dark Corner also had to deal with a third party known locally as the "out-layers." These individuals were men who were noted for switching sides at convenience and often striking out on their own to plunder the civilian population. The violence that spawned out of the struggle with the out-layers spanned the years after the War and culminated with the lynching of a notable out-layer leader at the Greenville County jail.[57]

The Civil War experience of the Dark Corner also helped to fuel the independence and lawlessness of the area. The community largely rejected the Confederate cause, as less than fifty men volunteered for service.[58] Along with refusal to participate in the Confederate war effort, the Dark Corner also developed into a notable refuge for Confederate deserters.[59] As conscripts from the mountains began to desert in mass, the community openly harbored them. Furthermore, the foreboding geography of mountains, such as Hogback, made for natural fortifications to resist against incursions by Confederate home guard looking for deserters. The level and organization of desertion was such that the chief enrollment officer for the northwestern counties of the State, Major John D. Ashmore, requisitioned field artillery in 1863 in hopes of suppressing the "treasonous" activities of the Dark Corner. However, his attempts to raze the various improvised fortifications that were thrown up in places such as "rocky-spur" and "hog-head" proved to be an exercise in futility.[60]

Unlike the Revolutionary War, where life returned to a more tranquil pace after the cessation of hostilities, the conclusion of the Civil War brought new struggles to the Dark Corner. As the Federal government began to exercise new authority in the South, the Dark Corner continued its refugee tradition. This time however, those who sought refuge were not seeking reprieve from the harassment of conscript officers; these individuals were trying to elude the "revenue officers." From the 1790s, the Dark Corner had become a haven not just for outsiders evading the law, but for those who were engaged in or were wanted for the crime of illicit distillation.[61]

The lawlessness that developed in the Dark Corner was not just a result of disdain for authority, but also an effect of the community's cultural connections to Appalachia. While newspapers labeled the Dark Corner as lawless, backwards, and murderous; the stereotype that developed was greatly exaggerated.[62] However, the Dark Corner was remote and had a well defined violence streak in its local culture, the ultimate root of the lawlessness was the desire to just be let alone and to practice self-determination free from outside interference. The Dark Corner residents used violence as a vehicle for a self-imposed rule of law in the area. Paired with another Appalachian trait, the distrust of outsiders, the Dark Corner had the potential to explode in reaction to outside interference with what they saw as the appropriate amount of resistance.[63]

Aside from culture and circumstance, geography contributed to the development of lawlessness in the Dark Corner. With the extreme expanses of what can be considered the Dark Corner spanning the remotest portions of three counties in South Carolina and wedged between the borders of two states, upwards of five separate law

enforcement agencies had potential jurisdiction over portions of
the Dark Corner. The remoteness of the Dark Corner from the
headquarters in Spartanburg and Greenville apparently created a sense
of apathy with many of the local agencies charged with enforcing the
law in the Dark Corner after the War.[64] Furthermore, the violent
reaction to incursions by law enforcement into the area, spurred
by the culture of the inhabitants, further dissuaded any effective
use of law enforcement. The only exceptions to this were those
law enforcement officers who had garnered popularity and respect
through fair and sensible uses of their authority.[65]

Adding to the different nature of the Dark Corner was the fact
that it was sparsely populated throughout most of the nineteenth
century. In 1875, for example, the Dark Corner had a population of
4,170 scattered throughout the largest four of the sixteen townships,
within Greenville County, none of which contained an urban
center. This number accounted for approximately 13 percent of the
county's total population.[66] The resulting wilderness feel of the Dark
Corner only fueled the continued practices of lawless, and further
complicated the enforcement of laws within the Dark Corner.[67]

Dark Corner inhabitants were notably different from their
counterparts in other portions of South Carolina during the
antebellum era. Instead of participating in the plantation slavery
system common to the lower elevations of the State, political and
social allegiances commonly found in the Dark Corner mirrored
political tendencies common to that of Appalachia.[68] Contrary to
many parts of South Carolina, the Dark Corner developed political
preferences that were generally based upon the reputation of the
candidate amongst the population, instead of loyalty based upon
party affiliation or political doctrine. This ultimately led to the
citizens of the Dark Corner supporting candidates that they had

personal esteem for, in spite of their party affiliation.[69] The Dark Corner's adamant support for unionist Benjamin Perry throughout his career is a prime example of how personal reputation could garner support in the Dark Corner.[70]

The political separation of the Dark Corner was in part fueled by its isolation from the changing economy of the Upstate. Viewed by many as a politically unenlightened portion of the State due to its unionist tendencies; the Dark Corner continued to remain an isolated political anomaly, even as other former unionist areas of the Upstate grew increasingly closer to the Lowcountry.[71] While much of the Upstate of South Carolina began to strengthen ties with the Lowcountry, both economically and politically, as the ante- and post-bellum cotton economy spread; the Dark Corner was another story.[72] As the hill country began to diversify into cotton and small time slave operations and post-emancipation tenant and sharecropping production, the mountainous regions of South Carolina were least affected by the development of the Upstate cotton economy as their production remained virtually non-existent.[73]

Furthermore, the Dark Corner was allowed to continue in its geographic and cultural isolation as it was sidestepped while much of the Upstate began to benefit from the development of an integrated internal improvement campaign.[74] While the Upstate began to increase its participation in the South Carolina market economy before the War, the Dark Corner remained largely subsistence based.[75] Dark Corner families continued to grow crops such as corn and wheat, with only a minimal investment in cotton for home consumption.[76] While other Upcountry farmers began to generate additional revenues with the growth of cotton and began to participate in the political defenses of the cotton economy, the families of the Dark Corner continued the economic system that had always been employed; subsistence farming and small-time home distillation. This economic avenue, tied with a geography that was less favorable for cotton production, left the Dark Corner the least affluent portion of Greenville County both before and following the War.[77]

Life by Any Means Necessary

As a result of increased economic isolation, the Dark Corner's production of alcohol increasingly became its most important source of revenue. The distillation component of the culture had its roots in the economy of the area at the earliest days of settlement. The families that settled throughout the Appalachians, most notably south of the Alleghany Range, quickly realized that grain cultivation provided the most consistent yield for cash crops. The highlands of Appalachia are not well suited for the traditional chattel slavery crops, such as cotton. However, livestock herding and staple crops such as cabbage, wheat, and corn flourish in the temperate climates. The cost and area needed to successfully manage a livestock operation, led many to undertake the cultivation of grains.

It goes without saying that corn is a bulky grain. The shape of the grain and the quantity in which it grows, presents a cumbersome challenge for transportation. Unlike un-milled wheat or rye that can be stuffed into a sack, the nature of corn does not afford the luxury of simplistic storage. Bulky sacks filled with a bushel of corn, simply will not stack or fit into a wagon in the same manner as the other crops. Due to the package space lost to the cumbersome shape of corn, undertaking the transportation of a sizeable amount of corn to a distant market would hypothetically involve a multitude of wagons and mule teams. With the precarious economic state of the typical mountain farmer in mind, it is easy to see that this presents a problem; most could not afford the multiple mule or oxen teams needed to move the large amounts of corn to market.

Due to the precarious state of Appalachian roads, the trip to market was quite an ordeal in some locations. Farmers leaving the Dark Corner bound for larger markets such as Asheville, Greenville, Pickens, or Spartanburg were confronted with a multitude of problems. Upon the farmer's arrival at the larger markets in the Upstate, they were quick to find that the laws of supply and demand dictated their yearly income. In bumper years, a buyer's market would have driven Dark Corner sellers to unload their crops at lower prices, resulting in a loss for the year.[78]

History shows us that another avenue was available to the Appalachian farmer. Whether it was the result of tradition and technology brought from the old world, or essentially borne out of necessity, the Appalachian farmer became privy to the art of distillation at a relatively early point in his economic development. Confronted with the pains of transportation and the lack of hard currency brought by corn on the open market, the Appalachian farmer turned to one of the oldest sciences in human history; the distillation of alcohol. By turning the starch in his grain into sugar, and the resulting sugar into alcohol, followed by the condensing of that alcohol into a more potent form; the Appalachian farmer was left with a product that was not only easier to pack through the mountain roads, but many times more valuable on the open market.[79]

During the last few decades of the nineteenth century, the alcohol market witnessed prices that fluctuated in the neighborhood of $1.10 to $1.20 per gallon; while raw corn went on the open market for a pittance of around half a dollar a bushel.[80] On average one bushel worth of corn meal could supply enough convertible starch for around fifty gallons of beer. It has been noted that the industry standard of the time was that fifty gallons of beer could be distilled into the neighborhood of three gallons of whiskey.[81] Therefore, a Dark Corner farmer who harvested twenty-five bushels could distill his crop into the neighborhood of seventy-five gallons of whiskey, and increase his profit exponentially.

This scenario, repeated countless times, became a yearly ritual that followed the autumn harvest. The "distilling season" usually ran from early September through later weeks of February, depending on the size of the crop and the type of product produced. This is not to say that distilling was not undertaken at other points throughout the year. However, this spike in distillation was largely the result of the necessity of making the most recent harvest into a more preservable form and the subsequent preparation for its use in barter for winter supplies.[82] While this practice was not the only economic venture afforded to the Dark Corner, it was certainly a very enticing one for those who made their living by farming in the area.[83]

Prior to the change in Federal liquor laws in 1866, the Dark Corner was actively distilling its grain.[84] However, as the political winds shifted after the Civil War and home distillation was outlawed, the Dark Corner soon became notorious for illicit distillation.[85] The level of distillation and the resulting lawlessness in the Dark Corner grew to such a point that at one time it was noted that, "blockade liquor is being made up in the corner with rankness and profession ... people who know say that it is impossible to receive a drink of clear water from any branch there, every stream being used for distillation purposes are more or less disfigured by distillery waste."[86]

In an exposé of the revenue problems that developed in the Dark Corner, a reporter from the *New York Times* spent time in Greenville amongst the moonshiners there. The reporter described a people that were indeed different from their modernized counterparts:

The moonshiner of the mountain region of North Carolina, South Carolina, Georgia, and Tennessee is a type found nowhere else… To the stranger he appears at first glance a very ordinary individual. He is generally long, lean, slow of speech, mild in manner, rough in dress and deportment, and apparently dull in intellect… The student of language will be delighted with his quant speech, abounding as it does in archaic and obsolete words handed down without the aid of books or manuscripts… he has preserved unimpaired the old English passionate love of personal freedom and home, and his unquestionable freedom to defend the latter even against the powers that be. He is English also in his readiness to resent an insult, and though he may lie occasionally, it is never safe to inform him of the fact.

All statute books in existence cannot persuade him that he has not a perfect right to make his corn into whiskey and sell it without interference in the shape of revenue taxes and deputy marshals… The laws against murder and manslaughter also are nullified by the moonshiner when deputy marshals become to inquisitive, when a neighbor turns informer and reveals to the officers the hiding place of a "still," and occasionally even when a stranger, whose business is not plainly evident and legitimate according to mountain ideas, ventures too far into the highlands… In the ethics of the mountains region no disgrace attaches to imprisonment for any of these offenses. Most men in every old moonshining district have been in jail for one or more short terms, but no one looks down on his neighbor on this account. Like sickness and death, it is simply a misfortune to which all are liable.[87]

Illicit distillation and the independent culture of the Dark Corner ultimately came to a head following the Civil War. Amidst the political turmoil of Reconstruction, a new struggle thus enveloped the Dark Corner. While trying to preserve its tradition of producing alcohol the Dark Corner would become caught up in a long and protracted armed struggle over self-determination and the role of the Federal government in the district. These prolonged conflicts were known as the "Revenue Wars."

Chapter Two

"All the Cunning and Blood-thirstiness of the Red Men": The Dark Corner Revenue Wars, 1866-1878.

A Marriage of Convenience

In early 1867 a Spartanburg county newspaper, the *Carolina Spartan*, ran a public announcement. While only a limited amount of type was devoted to the notice, the post heralded the start of a new era of unrest in the Upstate of South Carolina. Editors F. M. Wallace and E. M. Trimmer published the public notice of the new district collector, A.S. Wallace, and his intention to enforce the new excise tax to the most rigorous interpretation of the law:

> We observe that Mr. A.S. Wallace, the United States Tax Collector for this District, has issued a notice to distillers of sprits of any kind, warning all persons so engaged to desist at once, until they have conformed strictly to the law. The Revenue laws of the United States are very strict, and we have the assurance of the Collector, that he will enforce the law rigidly and strictly. It will be observed, that a license from the United States Tax Collector must be paid for. For the violation of these laws, the penalty is foreclosure of the liquor distilled, the vestals used, the boilers, the stills, and besides imprisonment not exceeding one year, and a fine of five hundred dollars. Preparations

are now making, to arrest every one who is carrying on this unlawful business. Surely those who have been and still are violating the law will now desist, rather than suffer the heavy losses they incur, thus bringing distress and misery on their families, We are informed that sufficient proof is already obtained against some of the persons, who have been carrying on this business for a long time- therefore take warning.[88]

Indeed the warning was taken by locals. The result was a major social upheaval. Accustomed to operating in a legal arena where the law could garner an illusion of respect, the deputy collector arrived in the Upstate of South Carolina with similar expectations for the population in the jurisdiction of his new assignment.[89] The Dark Corner would serve as an apt arena to test the metal of the new law and its chosen enforcers.

The law with which the new district tax collector had been charged to enforce had its roots in the Civil War.[90] Facing revenue shortages against an increasingly mounting war debt in 1862, the United States Congress introduced a series of revised excise taxes on many products, most notably tobacco and alcohol. After the cessation of hostilities, the Federal government made the temporary taxes on tobacco and alcohol permanent in 1866.[91] The Revenue Act of that year, called for a two dollar a gallon tax on all alcohol, and, as a result, targeted the basis of the Dark Corner's economy and some of the major tenets of its culture.[92] With the addition of government issued stamps in 1868, the series of laws not only created the modern tax system employed in the United States, but also laid the foundation for further postwar strife.[93]

The imposition of the excise tax came at a precarious time in South Carolina history. The confusion of Reconstruction created a situation in which enforcement of the new law was at times impossible. The transition between Confederate rebellion and Federal military rule left some of the remote sections of the mountains without the rule of law.[94] This situation left those charged with the enforcement of the revenue in a tight spot. Since any attempt to enforce the revenue in the remote portions of the mountain South was met with active resistance, the deputy collectors had to rely on the strength of the occupying Union army to enforce the new law.[95] This ultimately led to sympathy for those who were being pursued for revenue violations by those in other parts of South Carolina. Viewing the distillers as allies against a common enemy, the radical elements of the Republican Party; many former Confederate leaders throughout the state began to develop sympathies for the moonshiners and associate their local struggle with the greater struggle against the Reconstruction government.[96]

Over a decade since the cessation of hostilities and the end of South Carolina's final attempt at self-determination, it became ominously clear that the humiliation of Army occupation had no clear end in sight. The shared degradation of the protracted military presence forced many throughout the State to form alliances that were unimaginable during the antebellum years. Hungry for any opportunity to discredit the Reconstruction government, Redeemer politicians throughout the State threw their weight behind the cause of many notable moonshiners.[97] Both the former Confederates and the folks of the Dark Corner sought to remove Federal influence from their homes. The case of notorious distilling outlaw Lewis Redmond, and his relationship to Wade Hampton, was perhaps the most notable marriage of convenience.[98] In the struggle to take the state from the "interfering" Republicans, the self-rule movement accommodated men like Redmond as iconic figures.[99] However, the distillers would eventually outlive their usefulness and return to the fringes outside of "proper" southern society.[100]

The struggle over the postwar excise tax, which became known as the Revenue Wars, was an on-again, off-again, conflict that spanned the later decades of the nineteenth century and continued into the twentieth.[101] The Wars intensified seasonally, especially in the Spring and Fall, when distillers produced most of their liquor.[102] With an increased push in the enforcement of the revenue, the Revenue War in South Carolina hit a brutally intense point in the closing years of the 1870s. Initially, the campaign to collect money was successful because the earliest attempts at revenue enforcement came at the hands of Internal Revenue deputy collectors who had the support of Federal troops stationed in South Carolina.[103] However, when the Army occupation ended in 1877, the struggle intensified and became increasingly deadly for the revenue officers.[104] Without Army support, the situation in the mountains quickly deteriorated for the revenuers.[105]

One major problem for the deputy collectors lay in the original 1866 legislation that outlined the excise taxes on alcohol. In it, deputies were not allowed to destroy stills on site. Instead, the still had to be removed and destroyed under the auspices of the court. This error in judgment cost several deputy collectors their lives as elusive moonshiners ambushed several raiding parties that were distracted with the task of removing a still from a steep mountain hollow.[106] In desperate need of reinforcement, deputy collectors had to be accompanied by United States Marshals, in order to give them the warrantless arrest powers that they themselves lacked.[107]

Prior to the escalation in violence, the situation was not ideal. The show of force by the Army towards civilians, which in some cases resulted in deaths on both sides, led to the most effective enforcement of the revenue.[108] However, the use of occupying soldiers drew the wrath of the Redeemer politicians (those opposed to Republican rule) as well as the local inhabitants, and left the agents in an increasingly hostile situation after the Army withdrawal. [109]

Adding to the situation was the appointment of a new Commissioner of Internal Revenue, General Green B. Raum, who took office on August 2, 1876. Raum's tenure began close to the end of Army occupation in the South and the beginning of increased aggression against the revenue service in South Carolina.[110] He hoped to remedy the constant ambushing of Federal revenue agents throughout the South, most notably in northern Georgia and the Dark Corner.[111]

Raum brought effective organization to the service and was not timid in his use of force in the execution of the Revenue.[112] However, this new use of force was ineffective and only escalated hostility and violence toward the revenue agents. Even the militaristic organization created by Raum found itself victim to the tenacity of the moonshiners in the Dark Corner. Areas such as the Dark Corner and Northern Georgia were very dangerous for revenue agents. After years of ambushes, recaptured distilleries, and countless other acts of rebellion against the authority of the revenuers, in March 1879 Raum secured from Congress permission to destroy distilleries in the field. This move would ultimately protect his men and saved several lives.[113]

> **The practice of destroying distilleries in the field proved useful for the Internal Revenue Office. At first, the officers were content with disabling the distilleries with tools and axes. However, as the raids grew increasingly violent, dynamite was employed as a quick fix for larger tasks. Although it lost crucial evidence in cases against illicit distillers, the revenue officers could make a clean break from a raid without the danger of be-**

**ing tracked down from behind by a sympathetic party
of locals. Sworn testimony often made up for the lack
of copper in the courtroom. This practice ultimately
guaranteed ridding the Dark Corner of illicit distilleries. For the remainder of the Revenue Wars, this tac-
tic was employed on a regular basis**

With this change in command and a new direction of revenue
enforcement, the years 1877 through 1880 represented a watershed
in the Revenue War in South Carolina. This violent and tumultuous
time witnessed increased attempts at revenue enforcement by Federal
operatives, which in many cases met with disastrous results.[114] The
United States Marshals Office and the Internal Revenue Service
found themselves confronted with serious violence several times.[115]
Exacerbating the situation in its initial stages was the State of
South Carolina's refusal to help the Federal agents. Thus, with the
tacit approval of the State authorities in Columbia and Greenville,
the distillers in the Dark Corner took the offensive and left their
traditional territories in order to strike preemptively against the
revenue enforcers.[116]

The moonshiners of northwestern South Carolina found
themselves in an advantageous situation that allowed them to oppose
openly Federal authority in the State with little retribution from the
State itself.[117] The illicit activity of the Dark Corner provided the
Redeemers yet another opportunity to attack the Federal government
and its presence in the State. This political development only
encouraged the distillers, after having violently opposed the Federal
authority without retribution from the State it created a precedent
that encouraged Dark Corner resistance throughout the nineteenth
and early twentieth centuries.

An article appearing in Greenville's *Enterprise and Mountaineer* was indicative of the prevailing opinion toward the Federal presence in the Dark Corner. In an article acknowledging the difference between the inhabitants of the Dark Corner and the citizens of Greenville, the paper also expressed its concern that:

> **the shooting of still operators has gotten to be a common pastime with the U.S. Revenue Agents. We hope some of their infamous scoundrels may be brought to Justice for their murderous acts. We think it is a shame and disgrace to be a great nation like ours and to shoot them down like beast, the ignorant half civilized men who make a few gallons of whiskey while dishonest Revenue Agents go free.**[118]

The *Enterprise and Mountaineer* also published a letter from the *Abbeville Banner* that was quite sympathetic to the moonshiners:

> **I see a piece in the Enterprise and Mountaineer of this city copied from your paper, under head of "A Shame," upon the subject of the ignorant distillers of the upper country. It strikes me as most admirable piece and strikes at one of the greatest outrages that we have been forced to bear. If you will excuse me for the liberty I have taken, I will suggest in connection another great evil imposed upon these ignorant men, it is this-after being hunted down, and forced by files of United States soldiers, before and behind, handcuffed and lame with fatigue and travel, being compelled to move at an unnecessary rapid rate (old and young) they are sent to Charleston for trial, when we have a court in Greenville. I was a juryman last April, and the scenes I witnessed then were a disgrace to the country-poor ignorant men and boys tried by Negros and radicals without witnesses or counsel, two hundred and fifty miles away**

**from a soul they knew, except their fellow prisoners,
and convicted upon the testimony of a vagrant set of
United States officers It was simply horrible.**[119]

Here is a classic example of white solidarity in the postwar years.
The fact that a citizen of Abbeville, a lower piedmont town, would
express such outrage at the treatment of Dark Corner criminals
reveals much about the mentality of South Carolina whites during
this time. No matter who the white defendant was or where he came
from, it was still appalling to see the treatment that whites received at
the hands of "Negros" and Radical Republicans.[120]

The increased tension confounded Raum and the men who
served under him in the Internal Revenue Service. The ominous
situation was clearly outlined in a letter from a Republican-appointed
United States Marshal for South Carolina, Robert M. Wallace, to
United States Attorney General Charles Devens. In the letter dated
September 13, 1877, Wallace detailed the perplexing situation that
the revenue agents and his own men faced:

> **In order to facilitate the operations of the revenue
> officers I have given commissions as Special Deputy
> Marshals to nearly all of the Deputy Collectors in the
> State. Violators of the revenue laws in this State are
> very numerous and four fifths of the expenses of our
> courts go out to the enforcement of those laws- and
> if I would permit my deputies to prosecute all the
> violators which come to their knowledge the expenses
> of the District would largely exceed the limit fixed by
> your office.**
>
> **One of the most serious difficulties with which we have
> to contend is the universal hostility of the [D]emocratic
> State officials. They throw every possible obstacle
> in our way and if an officer in making an arrest or a
> seizure commits a technical violation of any State law,**

although he is acting in strict accordance with U.S. laws, he is at once arrested under a warrant from a trial justice.

In the mountain section of our State this active sympathy with law breakers is having its effect and officers do not dare to attempt to go there without combining from two or three counties and arming themselves thoroughly to meet open resistance and to protect members. Within the last three weeks two parties composed of Deputy Collectors and Deputy Marshals have been fired on in the mountains in Greenville County by parties engaged in illicit distilling and forced to retreat by the very men whom they went to arrest.[121]

According to Wallace, the Dark Corner was in such a state of active rebellion that a collective force of revenue deputies from three counties had been powerfully repulsed from the area. As a result, the increasing distillation arrests began to tax the Federal courts in South Carolina. Furthermore, the United States Marshals Office would be forced into bankruptcy if it tried to enforce the revenue laws to the levels that would be needed to suppress fully the illicit distillation. On top of this increasingly desperate situation, the Redeemer state government in power since that spring was hampering the Marshals' ability to exercise their Federal duties.[122]

As a result, 1877 was a costly year for Federal officers in South Carolina. At the beginning of the year, Raum faced a public relations nightmare when a revenue agent named Johnson shot and killed a small child being held by Jackson Ward, the very distiller he was sent to apprehend.[123] To make matters worse, Robert M. Wallace lost three men, all of them killed in the Dark Corner.[124]

The bloodshed was inaugurated on an exceedingly frigid night in early March. On the evening of the 12th, Hubbard Garmany, a fugitive from a Greenville County work farm, was preparing to transport a wagon load of liquor with his family along the Asheville Road. However, before Garmany could leave his own yard, the trip was abruptly ended. A local resident by the name of Van Buren Hendricks approached Garmany's house from the direction of the front yard with a pistol in hand, demanding that Garmany halt his mule team and step down from the wagon. Garmany anxiously obliged, dismounting the wagon but with arms full. One arm supported a young child across his chest, the other grasped a shotgun around the stock and trigger guard.

While neither a deputy marshal nor a revenue official, Hendricks blatantly disregarded both civility and the wellbeing of the child as he fired a shot in Garmany's direction without warning. The shot was answered by Garmany, the buckshot shredding Hendricks across the bowels. Hendricks dropped to his knees, and then slumped to one side. Amidst a cloud of rising vapors, as if his life was pouring from the various holes in his body, Hendricks died in the frozen and muddy ruts of Garmany's driveway.

The second incident occurred during the first week of June, when Deputy Collector Alfred McGregor was shot from a distance while plowing his cornfield after serving as the guide on a failed revenue raid in eastern Pickens County. While this cowardly assignation placed the revenue officers on edge, the occurrence was only the beginning of the troubles for the month.[125] These bloody affairs culminated with the murder of one of Wallace's former revenue officers in a small town in broad daylight.

On the sultry morning of June 12th, a train of prospective real-estate speculators boarded a flat in Spartanburg. Aboard this pleasure excursion was James Ledford, a notable local who sometimes moonlighted as a deputy collector. Upon arrival in Landrum, the northwestern Spartanburg town where the land auction was to take place, Ledford was confronted as he disembarked the platform. Three assailants grabbed Ledford by the collar and drug him onto the railroad grade.

There, in front of countless witnesses, the men savagely beat Ledford. Their grievance was a common one of those who had previous dealings with Ledford. As a deputy collector, Ledford's primary problem was that he was quick to shoot at fleeing or otherwise uncooperative suspects. The three men in question had all been fired upon in the preceding weeks. After extracting a satisfactory amount of physical retribution on Ledford, one of the men drew a pistol and fired several times into Ledford's torso while the remainder stabbed him with side knives. As Ledford lay dieing on the gravelly incline in the warm Appalachian sun, the crowd only looked on with worried fascination.[126] With the audacity of this murder in broad daylight and in front of dozens of witnesses, it appeared as if the moonshiners were taking the initiative in preemptively removing threats to their livelihood.

To compound the situation, Federal agents' abuse of citizens placed distillers in a favorable light with the majority of white South Carolina. This reality became evident when prominent South Carolina politicians voiced their support for the "king of the moonshiners," Lewis Redmond.[127] Redmond, originally from Transylvania County, North Carolina, had made a name for himself as an outlandish rebel who was the living embodiment of resistance to Federal Authority in the late 1870s.[128] Redmond's overt challenge to that authority; including successful distilling, the notorious murder of Deputy Collector Alfred Fuller Duckworth, deadly ambushes, and an audacious jail break in Pickens, was well known. His exploits provided the Redeemers with a Robin Hood stylized character behind which they could rally popular support.[129] However, eventually the moonshiners of the South Carolina mountains would find themselves alone in their struggle against Federal government tax collectors.

The opening distilling season of 1878 was even bloodier than the previous season for the Federal authorities in the Dark Corner. In April, word began to spread of a large distilling operation being conducted by Decatur Pace and Frank Turner just outside Tryon, NC. On the night of the 19th, a revenue party of eight members, under Captain A.C. Frey, slowly approached the still house under the cover of thickets. The raiding party was so artful in their approach that they managed to apprehend Frank Turner in the process of applying the final stages of his avocation by bottling the "backins," or the less potent runoff from his still, for use in a future run. Taken entirely by surprise, Turner surrendered his rifle and was sat next to the place were his still should have been.[130]

As a seasoned veteran of the moonshine war, Turner knew full well that following a successful run a distillery had to be removed from the still house in order to prevent its possible destruction in a raid. As an impromptu interrogation began, Turner became uncooperative for the first time, and refused to divulge the location of his copper. Frustrated by this development, Captain Frey ordered the members to spread out into the surrounding thickets in an attempt to uncover its location. Before the party cut out, two members were instructed to stay and watch Turner. Flem Moss, the party's guide, and a revenue officer by the name of Rufus Springs were left there to sit in the dark with their suspect. While Springs leaned against the side of the still house with his eyes affixed on Turner, Moss ventured inside to inspect the quality of the "backins." As Moss was in the midst of partaking in the low-grade libation, he heard a rifle shot ring out from the ridge. Cautiously looking out the door of the still house he saw Springs rolling on the ground exclaiming, "Lord have mercy, I am shot!"[131]

Panicking, Turner bolted from the still house and ran through a thicket. However, his instinctive choice in direction was not a good one as he ran headlong into a crowd of men, which he later testified was under the guidance of Decatur Pace. Turner managed to use the thicket as cover as the group opened fire on him, and as the men were loading their rifles, Turner made a break for the opposing ridge. Captain Frey and another revenue officer, Ben Ross, happened across Turner while they were carrying the recovered still pot down the opposite slope. By the time that the raiding party had consolidated and moved down to were the still house was, Turner was gone and Rufus Springs was dead. Hastily, the party abandoned the distillery and carried Springs' body down the mountain.[132]

While the Rufus Springs murder drew sympathies from local newspapers, such as the *Greenville Mountaineer*, no sympathy was found in the Dark Corner. Rewards were posted by the Marshals office, but to no avail. It took almost a decade to bring the suspect to trial, a local distiller, who was summarily found not guilty by the local jury.[133] This incident was not isolated, as very soon civilian informants who cooperated with Federal authorities discovered that they had also become targets in 1878.[134]

The significance of the Springs killing was clear; the Dark Corner was beyond control for the time being. Ideas abounded regarding the means to bring adequate revenue enforcement to the area. A few weeks after Springs' death, district attorney Lucius C. Northrop proposed that a small group of revenue officers, five or six at the most, should be used for a full time occupation of the Corner. This proposal was rejected because of the precariousness of the situation in that area.[135] Most revenue officers felt that if a full-time force was sent to occupy the Dark Corner, all of those sent would very likely be killed. Thus, by early May, the United States Marshals Office appealed to Governor Wade Hampton for help. In the minds of the Marshals office, the prevailing problem was the lack of communication and cooperation between State and Federal authorities. By 1878 Governor and former Confederate General Wade Hampton was willing to help, pledging full support and cooperation but only if some of the more objectionable practices, such as warrantless searches and seizures, were ceased.[136]

"The most fiendish, cold blooded murders ever committed in the county."

As a result, the good relationship between the moonshiners and the Redeemer government in Columbia was about to come to an end. As conditions began to change and a vision of the New South began to emerge, the moonshiner increasingly became viewed as a violent cutthroat.[137] The Redeemers, while at one time open to all sort of rebellion against the Federal authority in South Carolina, now began to shy away from those who donned the role of a Carolina Robin Hood.[138] This relationship of convenience would disintegrate further as the industrialists and boosters of local municipalities began to court northern investors.

While the alliance was quickly decaying, there was one last piece of support from a State authority. That summer, the State's fledgling cooperation with Federal authorities was shaken to its foundation. A case of mistaken identity and a questionable shooting by revenue officers will lead to one of the largest rebuffs of Federal authority since the Red Shirt crusades of the previous years.

On the second weekend of June, a party of revenue officers encircled and encamped along the woods that surrounded the house of Adeline Ladd. Adeline was the reputed concubine of one of the most wanted outlaws in the northwestern portion of the South Carolina, Lewis Redmond. Throughout the morning and afternoon of the 8th, the officers had kept close watch on the farm, in hopes of catching Redmond literally with his pants down. On the evening of the 9th, a man rode up to the farm and went inside. After a few hours, the party decided to rush the farm. Hugh Kane and William Durham charged the house from a blind side and then turned the corner towards the front door. Likewise, George Moose and Robert Scruggs hastily scrambled towards the house from the rear.[139]

Unfortunately for the officer's designs, Redmond was not in the house. The man they had seen enter the house was a close compatriot of Redmond and brother of Adeline, Amos Ladd. Reportedly, Ladd had come home to fetch iron implements for a blacksmith to repair. With the sack of tools in hand, Ladd opened the front door at the precise moment that the raiding party was ascending the front porch. As Ladd turned from facing his mother toward the front yard, he was shot square in the chest by Kane, who fired into him without announcement of his presence, warning, or legal warrant. Insisting that Ladd lunged towards him as he came into view from the blind side of the house, Durham also opened fire on Ladd, striking him twice with shots from his pistol.[140]

Following the impact of the bullets into his chest, Ladd dropped to his knees and slumped face down to the floor of the house. By all accounts, his left hand was still clasped onto the handle of the door as he died instantly. While his mother and sister shrieked out in rage against the horrible tragedy that had just unfolded before their eyes, the revenue officers were slowly beginning to realize what had just actually occurred. Quickly spotting an unloaded squirrel rifle next to the door, the resulting alibi developed like a whirlwind. As later

accounted in the officer's version of the incident, Ladd stormed out
of the house in a threatening manner. Armed with a rifle, Ladd fired
towards Kane. Luckily for Hugh Kane, the flint on the rifle refused to
answer and the shot was never discharged. In an admirable example
of reflexes and self preservation, the two officers cut down the
dangerous criminal simultaneously.[141]

While this story was spread throughout the news outlets, the
actions of the officers following the shooting were more telling of the
true nature of the incident. Leaving the farm directly following the
shooting and leaving Ladd's body where it lay, the party cutout to a
hillside to gather their senses. Knowing full well the gravity of the
situation, the party decided to split up. Kane traveled to Easley, while
Durham, Moose and Scruggs ventured onto the city of Greenville.
Following his arrival in Easley, Kane realized that Pickens County law
enforcement would most likely be looking for him in the morning
and decided to take a train to Greenville. Reunited with his fellow
party members, and informed via telegraph of a warrant issued by a
Pickens County trial justice, Kane suggested that the group surrender
to authorities. The group grudgingly agreed. Aware of the hostile
environment that was awaiting them in Pickens, the men surrendered
to Greenville County Sheriff Perry Duncan Gilreath.[142]

The incident garnered national attention. Newspapers throughout
the Upstate called for vindication in the name of Ladd. The *Pickens
Sentinel* reported that; "From all the facts gathered by us, we
pronounce this one of the most fiendish, cold blooded murders
ever committed in the county." Meanwhile, the South Carolina
Congressman for the 3rd district, David Wyatt Aiken, spoke out
against the killing and noted the gunman's northern flight would have
a negative effect on Federal enforcement in the mountainous portions
of the State.[143]

As the fallout from the Ladd shooting spread, the Federal authorities in the State quickly demonstrated support for their men. Aware of the conditions under which the raid was conducted, Ladd having taken part in the recent jail break of Redmond in Pickens County, Lucius C. Northrop outlined the difficulties facing his men in a letter to Attorney General Charles Devens:

> **I received a telegram advising me that Amos Ladd, of Pickens County, one of Redmond's gang and one of his party who broke jail had been killed by a party of Revenue officers composed of Deputy Collector Hugh Kane, Deputy Collector William H. Durham, G.W. Moose and R.P. Scruggs… The facts of the case may be summarized as follow: The act desperate and defiant violation of the Revenue laws. Even in this section is Lewis R. Redmond. He has not hesitated to add murder to his catalogue of crime and by the audacity of his recent rescue of this prisoner from the jail at Pickens CN, has attracted the attention of the Department… Redmond lives about 42 miles from Greenville and some 22 miles from Pickens in the heart of the mountains. The character of the country, the close laurel thickets, mountain peaks and passes, and the disposition of the people, as rugged as the rocks among which they live, make the attempt to secure Redmond or any of his gang a service of peculiar danger… They traveled in a wagon about 33 miles, abandoned the wagon and took the mountains on foot, working their way cautiously to the top of a peak in the rear of the house where Redmond's concubine and his children with her brother, the deceased, one of his most trusted henchmen lived. They waited and watched for a day, until on last Sunday morning about 10 O'C they concluded Redmond was in the house and prepared to charge the place. Deputy Kane advanced to the North side of the house and Durham to the South side. As Kane reached**

the open door he saw Amos Ladd, whose name is in the
warrant of arrest, standing there with his long flintlock
rifle in hand. He leveled his carbine and demanded sur-
render... Ladd pulled trigger, but his flint and steel re-
fused to reply and Kane fired upon him.[144]

Continuing his letter, Northrop reported that the officers initially
returned to Pickens before deciding to surrender in Greenville.[145]
Their reason for surrendering in Greenville was self-defense against
what awaited them in Pickens; a sure conviction at best, and at worst,
a lynching.[146] The Ladd killing demonstrated a primary problem
confronting revenue enforcers. The countryside was not safe and
if local suspects were killed in the line of duty, the revenue agents
were likely to be held legally responsible, assuming they lived long
enough.[147]

In a final attempt at continuing the mutual interest
between Redeemer and distiller, former Confederate
General, Judge Joseph B. Kershaw, railed against the
agents who he saw as hiding behind the constitutional
powers of the Federal government by using their com-
mission to evade "justice" at the State level. Judge Ker-
shaw wrote:

I have endeavored in the discussion to adhere strictly
to the points involved, but it is proper that I should
refer to a circumstance that sought to induce a careful
review of these acts removing for trial criminal cases
condescended in the State courts. They were passed in
times of great political excitement and during the most
serious disturbances of the relations between the States
and the government, Those of 1833 recommended by
General Jackson and adopted by Congress a part of the
celebrated "force bill," which was provoked by the as-

sertion of her sovereignty by the State of South Carolina, known as the "Nullification." That of 1866 was adopted at a time when the fiercest passions notoriously colored the legislation of Congress, and constitutional powers were stretched to the utmost limit, if not transcended, to reduce unto subordination the conquered States of the South. It would be natural that we should find amount the acts adopted at such periods and under such influences, imperfect and unconstitutional legislation...It is much better for the peace of society in the disturbed sections of the country, where these revenue troubles have prevailed, that I am enabled to reach that conclusion. Nothing tends more to maintain the supremacy of all laws and to enlist in their support of the hearty good will of the people, than the assurance of a regular, orderly and uniform administration of justice, through the regular and accustomed channel. On the other hand, the interposition of extraordinary and unusual modes of dispensing law and justice tends to shake the confidence of the people in the integrity of its administration. Nothing so effectively provokes lawlessness and disloyalty to all law.[148]

The motives behind Judge Kershaw's refusal to allow Federal jurisdiction to supersede that of the State were very clear. By equating the excise tax issue to South Carolina's state's rights campaign against "Tariff of Abominations," he effectively reflected the State's stance on Federal law enforcement in the South. Through Judge Kershaw, it became the State's opinion that while Federal law should be enforced, enforcement could not supersede state rights. While the Ladd murder was far from concluded in the justice system, the State had made its choice; her native sons and daughters were worth defending in the face of "rough" Federal agents.

The last vestige of defiance against the aggressive and arguably illegal attempts of the Federal authorities to superseded state authority came from Sheriff Gilreath of Greenville County. After two months of legal wrangling, it was decided that the case fell under the domain of Federal authorities. Following this controversial decision, United States Marshal for South Carolina R. M. Wallace took a party of deputies to the Greenville County jail and ordered Gilreath to open the cells holding the men suspected of killing Ladd. Gilreath denied the order and, seated at his desk, pointed to the wall. There hanging from the wall were the keys to the cells. Gilreath informed Wallace that he would not surrender his prisoners. In Gilreath's mind, if Wallace wanted those cells opened, he would have to do the honors himself.[149]

The situation in the Dark Corner, as well as in other regions of Appalachia, had turned the task of law enforcement into a publicity nightmare for the United States government. The failure to effectively enforce the tax in the first decade of its existence set the tone for the remainder of revenue enforcement. It remained a daunting task executed at great peril and cost. Nonetheless, some held out the hope of bringing the Dark Corner under control. In conversations about the revenue resistance, the authorities in Washington insisted on the recently and controversially elected President Rutherford B. Hayes that the situation in the Appalachian region of South Carolina was not as uncontrollable as it appeared:

> **At the meeting of the cabinet to-day, the trouble in South Carolina over the result of the revenue was up but not discussed at any length. In fact the question now raised is not considered so important as it has been represented in the newspapers. Commissioner Raum says: "The whole matter has been grossly exag-**

gerated for political purposes."[150]

However, Raum was wrong, as the situation in Northwestern South Carolina was not over exaggerated. The fact of the matter was that for the time being, the Internal Revenue Office had been losing serious ground in the mountains of South Carolina. If the situation was to be remedied, unprecedented action had to be taken. In August 1878, Raum did just that. He proposed a series of regulations that would amount to general amnesty for low level non-violent offenders throughout the country.

Clemency

According to Raum's plan, small-time offenders who willingly surrendered to authorities and were able to pay the cost of court would be allowed to return home and serve a sentence through probation. This was a significantly more generous offer than that which had become the norm; a one hundred dollar fine and two months hard labor. While selected amnesty had been experimented with under President U. S. Grant's administration with mixed results; the general clemency offered by Raum had the potential to end the armed resistance to revenue agents since the distillers would have a favorable alternative to prison.[151]

Sympathetic to the plight of the mountain farmer, the initial response to clemency was welcomed by some in the Dark Corner. In early August over one hundred fifty distillers surrendered under the new offer.[152] While this was encouraging, those still engaged in revenue enforcement were less than confident. In a letter to Charles Devens, United States Marshal Robert M. Wallace expressed his disappointment with the latest developments:

> I was surprised when I heard the announcement of
> the District Attorney. I doubt the success of this plan
> for correcting the abuses of the law. It will succeed in
> some cases but I believe that it will fail to accomplish
> the desired end among a majority of the hostile viola-
> tors of law. Nothing but the fear of punishment will
> work upon the feelings of many of the ignorant and
> vicious people engaged in distilling in the mountain
> regions.[153]

Indeed, Wallace's experience with the distilling population of
the mountains was not a pleasant one. After losing three men the
year previous, having agents fired upon earlier that year, the notable
jail break of a notorious offender, and the publicity nightmare of
the Amos Ladd killing, it is easy to understand Wallace's skepticism
about the new clemency offer. However, Wallace had some practical
concerns about the offer and how it was to be implemented. In the
same letter, Wallace brought to Devens attention:

> Nothing was said in reference to the payment of cost
> and the impression was made on the public was that no
> cost were required to be paid. The announcement was
> hailed until men who had been engaged in various vio-
> lations of law and nearly all defendants, even the most
> guilty, asked to be allowed to enter the plea of guilty
> and after this morning one hundred and sixty five had
> registered their names for that purpose.[154]

The flood of violators and uniform implementation of the
clemency must have cut Wallace to the marrow. The mishandling
of the offer led many to view the clemency as a loophole that the
roughest violators could use to avoid prosecution.[155] It was true,

however, that many throughout the Southern Appalachians took advantage of the clemency offering. In the Dark Corner alone, Wallace admitted that over a hundred and sixty five violators surrendering due to the clemency offer in the first week. For the first time, there was a real hope of a peaceful resolution to revenue enforcement.

On the surface, it may appear that the Dark Corner had learned some respect for the law. In a sense this was true. However, in their experiences with the Internal Revenue Office over the previous twelve years, the distilling population of the Dark Corner had learned to recognize an opportunity to avoid the law when it presented itself. The more realistic members of Raum's administration, such as Marshal Wallace, believed the clemency would only postpone additional violence.

According to Wallace, the revenue agents would have to deal with these offenders again in the future and that these offenders would be looking for yet another issue of clemency once in custody. It was his opinion that only a sufficient use of force, the strong arm of the law, and the stiffest fines and punishment would bring an end to the revenue violators. Wallace's experiences with the mountain regions of South Carolina had brought him to the conclusion that force was the only answer. Any offer of clemency would only allow the distiller enough breathing room to better organize his next attempt at breaking the law. Force, however, was clearly having little effect in areas such as the Dark Corner.[156]

Contrairy to Wallace's expectations the policy was working. Lucius C. Northrop reported that the show of leniency was effectively the first step in cementing the authority of the Federal government over the mountain populations of the State. Indeed, the 1878 clemency offer was a breaking point within the Revenue War, as the

Internal Revenue Service began to garner support from those who believed in the New South. The clemency offer had served as an olive branch to the modernized and law abiding citizens of the Upstate. It was Northrop's opinion that the show of restraint by revenuers toward citizens who were once hostile would make the modernized citizens of the Upstate willing to offer assistance to the deputy collectors, as well as sponsor those who willingly surrendered[157]

The clemency offer made in 1878 was the turning point in the public perception of revenue enforcement in South Carolina. Prior to the offer, the enforcement of the revenue in South Carolina had been a serious struggle. The War seemed unwinnable, as the Redeemer government sided with the revenue resistance in the mountains. However, following the offer, the revenue agents were able to exploit the moral high ground as lenient and forgiving representatives of the law. Their offer was indeed generous; plead guilty, pay court costs, and pledge to cease all violation. From this point forward, the revenue agents in South Carolina could draw sympathy in the face of continued rebellion and attacks by hostile inhabitants in the mountains. From the late summer of 1878 forward, in most cases the revenue agent was now perceived as the moral character in the struggle and the Dark Corner moonshiner as the antagonist. While there were numerous flare-ups about the methods of revenue enforcement employed by the various Federal agencies; the blockaders never again enjoyed the popular support which they had garnered from 1877-78.

The clemency, ultimately, did not end the Revenue Wars. A shortage of funds had plagued revenue enforcement. Ironically, this was largely because of the clemency offer of the previous year. The root of the problem was that revenue officers were paid by the arrests they made during a bust.[158] Since not as many arrests were being made in the mountain regions, deputy agents who made their pay via commission were going without. In a letter to Charles Devens, Lucius C. Northrop addressed the situation by stating that "If the officers are not paid, they will not work and the service may suffer and I am therefore of the opinion that it is better to arrest the party and upon payment if the Commissioners cost and correction of the wrong to drop the prosecution, than to suffer the law to be violated in its lightest regiment."[159]

By 1879, it was clear that the humane approach to the illicit distillation problem did not make for sound business. During this year, the United States District Attorney for South Carolina argued that the revenue service should commence the same notorious raids of small time operators with little leniency; the exact practices that had manifested into the violent nightmare of the previous years. While the revenuers had the upper hand morally and politically in South Carolina, practices such as aggressive still raids, coupled with the love/hate relationship of Federal authority in South Carolina, led to the protracted conflict within the mountainous portions of the State. For the next five decades, it would seem that every time the Internal Revenue Service tried to step up enforcement, the Dark Corner slipped further into lawlessness. However, the inhabitants of the Dark Corner faced a more serious challenge to their way of life; the New South booster from within their own region.

Figure 1: Homesteads such as this one were common to the Appalachian Mountains and to the Dark Corner. The topography and relative poverty of the inhabitants kept most of those who resided in the Dark Corner out of the chattel slavery economy. (Library of Congress)

Figure 2: Hogback Mountain as seen from Vaughn's Gap. The very rapid rise in elevation found in the Northwestern extremes of South Carolina makes the topography of the majority of the Dark Corner unsuited for large scale agriculture. (Collection of Beau Blackwell)

Figure 3: This illustration demonstrates the growing fascination with the Revenue War wagged throughout Southern Appalachia in the last decades of the nineteenth century. Often violators were unfairly painted as backwards, simpleminded, and murderously aggressive. (Library of Congress)

Figure 4: The hazards of illicit distillation and the dangers of revenue enforcement were well known to both camps of the conflict. Those charged with enforcing the revenue routinely orchestrated ambushes for unsuspecting distillers along roadways and in hallows. Likewise, moonshiners were notorious for protecting their investment with demoniacal aggression. (Library of Congress)

Figure 5: Revenue officers in the Dark Corner were notoriously aggressive. Here a revenue party had conducted an extralegal expedition into Transylvania County, North Carolina to apprehend a suspect wanted in South Carolina. (Courtesy of the Pickens County Museum.)

Figure 6: Trial dates for moonshiners were exercises in inconvenience. Prior to offers of amnesty, suspects usually arrived at the court house with the expectation of a few months worth of service on a prison farm to look forward to. This left the distiller's family with both financial and emotional burdens during the absence. (Library of Congress)

Figure 7: This illustration depicts a typical distillation camp common to the Dark Corner during the period of the Revenue Wars. (Library of Congress)

Figure 8: This illustration outlines the common pot still that was employed during the heyday of the Revenue War in the Dark Corner.[160] (Courtesy of Rebecca Saunders)

Figure 9: The production of illicit alcohol in northwestern South Carolina did not end with the Revenue Wars of the nineteenth century. Operations such as the one pictured here were commonly found throughout the Dark Corner well into the 1970s. (Courtesy of the Pickens County Museum)

Figure 10: Here the arresting officers pose for a photograph in front of the aforementioned still. (Courtesy of the Pickens County Museum)

Chapter Three

"When their anger is stirred nothing is too low for them to do": The Dark Corner and the New South

The Rise of the New South and Temperance in Greenville

As South Carolina took the first steps away from its agrarian past after the Civil War, the Dark Corner continued its antebellum economy of subsistence farming and production of illicit alcohol. The failure to follow the State's path toward an industrialized, modern, and sober future drew negative attention from New South boosters in the Upstate. While these boosters of the Upstate constantly tried to attract new industry into their region, they also took strides to rein in the more wild elements of their communities. The end result was a public relations campaign that simultaneously boasted the pious and industrious habits of Greenville, and condemned the uncouth and rustic habits of those in the Dark Corner.[161]

The Civil War had demonstrated to some in the South that the industrial development of the North had been one of the major deciding factors in the conflict.[162] The lessons learned in the War were very influential in the decision to pursue industrialization and modernization.[163] South Carolina began its industrial push under the Reconstruction government. By 1886, the State had joined many of its fellow southern states in drafting laws that ensured that new capital investments in industry were all but exempt from taxes on capital.[164]

This new embrace of industrialization paid off, as the number of cotton operations in South Carolina quadrupled between the early postwar years and the early twentieth century. By the early 1900s, the greater piedmonts of the Carolinas had surpassed their northern counterparts in production and spindles, thus taking the lead in the manufacturing world. Truly the "Cotton Mill State" of South Carolina was exploding with new operations, and factory towns were transforming the traditional population centers of the Upstate.[165]

During the 1880s and 1890s, the city of Greenville found itself the second largest concentration of cotton spindles in South Carolina; just short of the number found in Spartanburg.[166] But in many ways, Greenville had surpassed its neighboring city. It was host to many of the purchasing agents for the industry, as well as numerous cotton mills, and it was the point of delivery for many of the industry's supplies.[167] The industrial renaissance had occurred seemingly by accident. Although Greenville could boast a railroad since 1853, and it was the home of a few small operations spread throughout the county, the Great Boston Fire of 1872 was the catalyst for the birth of its cotton mills.[168]

Following the fire, northern industrialists Oscar H. Simpson and George S. Hall relocated their firm there. They did so to take advantage of the cheap southern labor and non-existent labor laws.[169] The northern counterparts of the Carolina "lint heads" had begun to unionize and create unwanted headaches for their business leaders. The natural remedy to these troubles was to relocate to the South, where workers were willing to take on a full array of hazardous work for mere table scraps.

With the influx of formerly northern based operations, South Carolina's industrialization continued to grow at the expense of her labor force. As South Carolina's spindles grew over 151 percent in the 1890s, the work week did as well. In many cases in South Carolina, it was in excess of seventy hours.[170] Furthermore, child labor laws were practically nonexistent. In 1887, Alabama led the way with a law that limited child labor to an eight hour day. However, that law fell victim to industrialist pressure and was struck from the books in 1895.[171]

The proponents of the New South and industrialization seemed to be having their unencumbered way with the workers of South Carolina. The only remnants of self-expression that hindered the industrialist's total control of the population was their lack of influence over their workers' morals and minds.[172] The push for sober morality in the factories of the Upstate was an attempt to create a more devoted workforce.[173]

As the definition of mill town life began to take shape, it became clear that the low wage workers and their families could be manipulated into morality through adjustment of the social environment.[174] This push for morality by industrialists led ultimately to it being synonymous with economic success and New South development. The key component of the moralist push, temperance, would become a pillar of this new southern development and once again place the Dark Corner outside of the Carolina mainstream.[175]

After the Civil War, local newspaper editors and politicians throughout the major urban centers of the South began campaigns to turn their antebellum burgs into booming modern metropolises. Part of the boosters' difficult task was shading investors from the undesirable elements of their communities.[176] The great hurdle the progressive New South boosters of Greenville had to overcome was the "backward" elements of their county.[177] The booster spirit found in Greenville was the result of the belief that their communities were common enterprises.[178] The only effective way to entice industry was to sell the community. Aside from a workforce, Greenville had to be able to trump a community that was clean and hospitable. In a sense, Greenville had to transform itself into the natural seat for the development of further industry and investment.

Indeed, the business leaders of communities throughout the Upstate ventured into politics for this very reason. The most direct example of this transformation was the tenure of one Greenville mayor. During the 1880s, Samuel A. Townes sought office with the intention of renovating the city in order to facilitate trade for his dry-goods business. His tenure saw the construction of a new city hall and the creation of a city board of health.[179]

Structural construction and renovation were not the sole tasks confronting the boosters. They also had to mold the populous of Greenville into an obedient and clean workforce that would facilitate industry into the city.[180] Drawing from the paternalist antebellum South Carolina society, the boosters and the industrialists believed that they could largely implement their will on society for its betterment.[181] As one later industrialist, Ben Greer, put it more succinctly: "Our mills shall run not only to make cotton cloth, but to make the right kind of men and women as well."[182]

Luckily for the boosters, their task afforded them the moral high ground of the late nineteenth century. Temperance and the Christian virtues of obedience were tools that they could employ to control the masses and drive them into the progressive camp.[183] The notions of temperance also afforded a common connection to the local middle-class and professional community, who were at the heart of the booster movement.[184] Together, the social elites, industrial capitalists, boosters, and obedient workers could ride high on a temperance wave that would wash the less desirable elements out of their beloved foothills city and usher them into a bright future.[185]

The attack from the New South boosters on the less desirable elements had two focuses; the poorer inhabitants of the city and the "unruly" rural inhabitants of the county, especially the Dark Corner. The first part of this campaign was to champion temperance and prohibition. By continually running stories in the local newspapers about the evils of drink and the benefits of prohibition, the New South editors documented the "good fight" and the successes of other communities who chose to rid themselves of the evil of alcohol.[186] The second part came in the form of scapegoating the undesirable elements in the county.[187] Through the power of public ridicule and "proper" education, the editors hoped to sway public opinion to their camp.[188]

The temperance agenda of the papers was clear from early on. While not the only temperance minded paper in the Upstate, the *Greenville Mountaineer*, which saw itself as "a conservative journal and reflex of popular events," was certainly one of the most vocal papers concerning the temperance question.[189] Temperance had always been a mainstay of the editorials, the combination of modernization within the county and the quickly expanding moonshine war in the 1870s made the issue even more pertinent. In an attempt to boast Greenville as one of the enlightened cities of the South, the paper adopted the mantel of temperance and prohibition as its own and ferociously cut into the "rough" elements of the county.[190] Naturally, a large volume of this assault was directed towards the Dark Corner.

In 1870, O.E. Elford, the editor of the *Enterprise and Mountaineer*, outlined the frustration of the temperate progressives in the "fair" city following a failed movement to have prohibition passed by the city council:

Without any intention of attempting to discuss the
question of temperance, for that has already been
done most ably and thoroughly. I wish to express
what I believe to be the general sentiment of the good
people of Greenville County, upon the failure of the
effort to prohibit the sale of liquor in Greenville City.
Scarcely, any thing has occurred for years which has
so much interested the people throughout the entire
County, and be assured the result of the election is the
source of profound regret and real pain to them. We
love the City of Greenville, we love her institutions
of learning, her churches, her factories, we are proud
of her progress and growth, but we are sad to think
that all there are to be hampered, and crippled for
another year by that great evil-bar rooms with their
wide spread influence for evil and only evil and it is
most painful to know that indifference on the part of
a number of prominent citizens and business men of
the City was largely the cause of failure on the part of
that noble band of men and women who have labored
so long and so earnestly to stamp out this fire whose
lurid, deathly glare has fallen in so many happy home
circles and which is surely burning its way into so
many human hearts.[191]

The frustration of Elford about the election was made clear in his
editorial. This article, while not the inaugural piece of the progressive
newspapermen's campaign against drink, did sum up the political
situation in Greenville. While not discounting the morality behind
the issue, the editors were anti-drink for the benefit of the city herself.
By being a progressive city, benefiting from a strategic location, an
agreeable climate, generous boosters, and a pious populous; the city
of Greenville could only stand to continue its development. This

argument was continued time and time again by city boosters.[192] Ultimately, the temperance and prohibition cause began to grip the city and the county. Anybody opposed to temperance increasingly bore the brunt of the social stigma of being outside community standards.[193]

The temperance overtone of the paper hit such proportions that the editors "outed" those active in the distillation economy. Starting in the summer of 1870, the *Greenville Enterprise* began following the developments of the circuit court and listing the names and infractions of those convicted of illicit distillation. Systematically listing the offender, the crime, and the punishment became ever present aspect of coverage. While some of the crimes were not liquor related, the vast majority were men and women found in violation of excise taxes. The public chastising of those convicted of distillation continued through the merger with the Greenville based *Mountaineer*. The architects of opinion in Greenville showed open hostility toward those who lived in the Dark Corner.[194]

The temperance campaign in Greenville accelerated in October 1872 as the Greenville Division of the Sons of Temperance formed at the county courthouse.[195] From its inception, the temperance movement within the city of Greenville wanted prohibition. However, the movement continually failed to convince the population through the 1870s and 1880s.[196] In February 1884, however, the creation of a chapter of the Women's Christian Temperance Union in Greenville signaled that political winds were shifting against Greenville's tradition of alcohol consumption. Under the guidance of the boosters and the now widespread temperance organizations, Greenville as a whole moved towards strict regulation of alcohol. In the 1892 statewide referendum for prohibition, the city of Greenville cast 1,545 votes for prohibition and only 1,016 against the measure.[197]

However, the biggest hurdle to prohibition's success came when the State Dispensary was formed by Governor Benjamin R. Tillman in 1893, as a possible compromise that would pacify both the "dry" and "wet" as well as generate revenue.[198] Ever the vigilant politician, Tillman had been wary of the divisions developing within his voting block over the temperance issue. As temperance and prohibitionist factions throughout the State began to gain momentum, some farmers in his coalition objected to the suppression of alcohol. Tillman's response, a state monopoly on the production and sales of alcohol, was intended to cement his power base by unifying the two sides of the argument, while simultaneously expanding the power of the State.[199]

However, the Dispensary was not the great unifying law that Tillman had hoped it would be. Resistance to the Dispensary was widespread throughout the State. Underground activity, such as the establishment of illegal speakeasies known as "blind tigers," resulted in active resistance, culminating in the events known as the Dispensary War.[200] The fallout of Dispensary resistance was felt throughout the State.[201] In Greenville and Spartanburg, constables were kept busy with raids on underground barrooms.[202] In the Dark Corner, Dispensary agents were attacked with the same fervor that was usually reserved for revenue officers.[203] The climax of the struggle came in Darlington, in the Pee Dee region of the State, where a full fledged rebellion developed.[204]

Following Tillman's election to the United States Senate in 1895, the Progressive movement in South Carolina took an interesting turn. Tillman pursued mildly Progressive initiatives, highlighted by his verbal assaults against the money interest in Congress and by the articulation of his deep distrust of large employers.[205] However, the movement would be stymied by South Carolina's new governor, Coleman Blease. Blease's tenure as governor, which was characterized by support of the lower-class and free labor laws for industrialists, facilitated the need for greater progressive reforms within the State.[206] Of these reforms, the most profound was Governor Richard Manning's push for statewide prohibition under the medicinal gallon a month law in 1916, which was later altered to one quart a month in 1918.[207]

As a result of the new ethos in most of Greenville County and the State, the Dark Corner's resistance to outside authority became the topic of much fascination within the city of Greenville.[208] At the same time that the city was building its reputation as a civilized and progressive example of the New South, the Dark Corner was beginning to gain notoriety as a backwards community desperately clinging to its heritage.[209] By the latter decades of the nineteenth century, the cultural paradox had been solidified. The consensus was clear; Greenville County was too small an area to support two such profoundly opposite visions of the future. Therefore, the Dark Corner had to be enlightened and dragged into the bright future of the New South; a New South which newspaper editor Henry Grady had declared in the 1880s was "in love with work."[210]

A People of No Account: the Booster Assault on the Dark Corner

The Dark Corner was a growing thorn in the side of the boosters. Once quieted by "amnesty," the Dark Corner rose again in the 1880s and 1890s.[211] By 1890, the violence had grown to such a level that it demanded even more of the attention of the Greenville boosters. Dark Corner violence was the very sort of publicity that could destroy the image of the New South. After all, major industrial capital would never locate in a county that could not control its undesirable elements. In the boosters' opinion the Dark Corner needed to be addressed. As a result, local newspaper men began to describe the Dark Corner as an anomaly; a backwards community full of cutthroats wholly unattached to Greenville and a burden to the development of the county.[212] Starting in the late 1870s, the editors began to publish any and all accounts of action in the Dark Corner. The reports outlined an uncivilized community that was bent on preserving its unfortunate habits through violence and murder.[213] And, unlike during Reconstruction, the elites of Greenville began to accept the idea of Federal intervention within the mountains of their county.[214]

However, the boosters of Greenville were not alone in their campaign against mountaineers. There were other proponents of the New South in the State that shared similar opinions. The editor of *The State* newspaper in Columbia, Narciso Gonzales gave his opinion of Dark Corner men by noting that, for the men of the mountains, "law held no terrors for him, religion presented no attractions and education was unheard of altogether."[215] With such scathing accounts of the residents of the mountains, it is clear that the New South boosters in Greenville had allies in their campaign to reform or at least isolate the Dark Corner.

Although there had been some sympathies against the harsh enforcement and treatment that the inhabitants of northwestern South Carolina received in the early days of the revenue enforcement campaign, any such sympathies had long since evaporated by the 1880s. The level of disgust and change in sympathy is evident in the tone of an article that Spartanburg based editor T.H. McMahan wrote about the assassination of a government distiller, turned revenue official, in Glassy Mountain near the Spartanburg county border in 1888:

> A deplorable state of affairs exists in this locality. Just after dark, Thursday night, Ben Ross a well known government distiller and liquor dealer at Glassy Mountain, was laying down on the floor before the fire of his house, when someone came up to a glass window and fired… The whole contents of a shot gun were fired into his breast and bowels as he lay facing the window… The inquest was being held Friday, and no attempts were being made to arrest or find out the guilty parties, and witnesses were afraid to testify what they knew. It was a regular organized band in there, armed with 16 shooters and double barreled shot guns and it was not safe for any man to ride through there. The whole neighborhood is entirely under the control of the blockaders. The trouble seems to have arisen in this way: Ross was selling government whiskey at $1.50, and the blockaders at $1.00, and from that a bitter feeling arose between them which led to trouble, reporting, threatening, etc., until the parties were constantly looking for each other with double barreled shot guns loaded with buck shot. It is right in this place where Elkin was shot, and where Ladson was shot, and where Brown, Aiken, Dill, and Hightower were shot so recently. The Greenville officers will not dare go in there to make any arrests.[216]

In a complete reversal from the argument made by editors prior to 1877, McMahan continued:

> I shall listen to see what is going to be the result, and see if the authorities of this government both State and United States, are going to allow this state of af-

fairs to go on and make no effort to bring the guilty to justice.[217]

The widespread observance of the New South doctrine in the Upstate created a watershed in political thinking. In the not too distant past, State and local leaders had railed against the strong use of Federal law enforcement in their communities and the resulting abuses thereof. Now, as industrialism took over the Upstate and ties to northern capital became stronger, editors were now arguing that the Federal government was not doing enough to bring law and order into their communities.

Similar sentiments were echoed by McMahan's Greenville counter part. In a follow-up editorial to the assassination, John C. Bailey of the *Enterprise and Mountaineer* expressed his rancor towards the Dark Corner:

> **Last week we published the main facts in the killing of Benjamin A. Ross in Glassy Mountain Township of this County. It was one of the most cowardly and murderous assassinations that has ever occurred in Greenville. We think Governor Richardson should at once offer a suitable reward for the detection of the person or persons engaged in committing the crime. The wildest part of the West could exhibit no more wanton disregard of law and order.**[218]

Perhaps the situation was best defined in a letter to the editor expressing the need for a new and larger courthouse. Otis Mills, a recent foreman on a district court jury, wrote an editorial for the *Enterprise and Mountaineer*. In it, Mills vented frustration in the mounting case loads and cramped conditions of both the district courthouse and the accommodations of the local Internal Revenue office. Clearly, while Greenville was growing, the Dark Corner was itself expanding the level of its illicit activities.[219]

The Dark Corner situation continued to tarnish the mantle of the New South boosters in Greenville. The notoriety of the Dark Corner grew to such an extent that the boosters sought to segregate themselves from the inhabitants. By clearly establishing that the Dark Corner's only tie to Greenville was through geopolitical borders, the boosters could separate the Corner's stigma from their good name. In a newspaper article from 1894, the editor of the *Greenville Daily News* wrote:

> **The Dark Corner declares itself independent and paddles its own canoe--blockade stills on all sides-- experience of a raiding party in pursuit of two men wanted for murder-traps set in mountain ravines and laurel thickets and what came of them--fi[er]ce dogs and trained fowls on guard--a blockade declaration of purpose and program.**

> **The Dark Corner section of Greenville County has seceded from the United States of America and is now an independent country. As soon as the boys have a little spare time they will probably throw up fortifications, hoist a flag and formally demand recognition from the great powers. The form of government is simple. Every man is his own boss and is expected to take care of himself. The authority of Sheriff Gilreath is yet recognized because he is personally popular, but B.R. Tillman and Grover Cleveland are out of date, and persons representing them may expect to be regarded and treated as suspicious strangers. Blockade liquor is being made up in the corner with rankness and profession which is refreshing and people who know say that it is impossible to receive a drink of clear water from any branch there, every stream being**

used for distillation purposes ad more or less disfigured by distillery waste... What with that natural advantage, the impenetrable thickets, steep mountain sides, and deep ravine, the sharpness of the mountain people and the enthusiastic fi[er]ce dogs and educated fowls, a successful invasion of the Dark Corner is rather a complicated and doubtful job.
Ten people have been killed and a dozen or more badly hurt in the corner in the last three years and nobody has been punished. The theory seems to be that so long as it is Dark Corner people who kill Dark Corner people nobody outside has any reason or right to interfere.[220]

The violence in the Dark Corner had grown to such a level that it was actually worse than the 1870s "Wars." This time the complaints about the lawlessness were not coming from Federal authorities, but instead were coming from local leaders. Ironically, the section of the county that had most ardently opposed secession and the Confederate government was saddled with the label of "secessionist." However, this was not a political secession in any conventional sense. As the New South editors saw it, this was as an economic and cultural secession.

The message was clear. The progressive New South boosters of the city were tired of the constant barrage of unsettling news from the Dark Corner. Ripe with frustration, the editor portrayed the unruly section of the county as an independent nation seeking autonomy. However, there was some truth in their editorials. The people in Dark Corner had exercised a relatively healthy amount of autonomy since its original settlement. In their eyes, their affairs could be managed within the community. The constant influx of outsiders enforcing "foreign" laws had driven the Dark Corner to arms since the 1860s. Even at the turn of the century, the inhabitants continued to ignore the liquor laws. For example, in 1898 Captain H.W. Harp of the Internal Revenue Service made his frustration and opinion towards the inhabitants of the Dark Corner known when he was interviewed by a reporter of the Spartanburg based *Piedmont Headlight*. The reporter adequately summed up Harp's frustration when he wrote:

> **Stills around Glassy Mountain were almost as thick as fleas in a hog pen, and every secluded branch was utilized by moonshiners. The revenue officers are constantly making raids and cutting up the "coppers", but when one still is destroyed two others are at once set up…We asked Captain Harp why the officers didn't remove the stills after capturing them? He replied that it was as much as a man's life was worth to attempt such a thing. When a raid was made in the Dark Corner the officer's had to work like fighting fire, and get out before the alarm could be given or they would be ambushed and shot into ribbons…Captain Harp says if a man don't believe those Glassy Mountain moonshiners will shoot, he had better go up there and tackle them, and his mind will be quickly disabused. They have no more compunction of conscience about shooting down a revenue officer than they would a rabid dog, and as their neighbors are either in sympathy with the blockaders, or afraid of them, it is hard work to apprehend or arrest a violator of the law. Captain Harp says that many of those Glassy Mountain moonshiners have Indian blood in their veins and possess all the cunning and blood thirstiness of the red men.**[221]**

Like so many others, Harp painted the mountaineers as vile criminals. Harp noted that the mountaineers of the Dark Corner intended revenue agents harm due solely to their opposition to the tasks called for while performing their sworn duties. Murder was just

a hazard of the enforcement of the Revenue Laws and was expected
when working amongst such "backward" men and women. While
there were violent reactions to the Revenue Law in other portions of
the Appalachians, the Dark Corner had complete community support
for the liquor industry, and that separated it from other enclaves of
revenue resistance.[222]

The negative interpretations of the Dark Corner did not end
with the nineteenth century. While some families from the Dark
Corner had begun to migrate to the cotton mills, little changed in
the community.[223] In the opening decades of the twentieth century,
the boosters of Greenville were just as adamant about the ferocity of
the Dark Corner as were their predecessors. In a 1906 article about
a reprisal assault on a local magistrate, the *Greenville Daily News*
observed:

> **"Moonshiners" some of whom are yet to be found in
> the Dark Corner, have a peculiar idea of what consti-
> tutes revenge. When an injury, or at least what they
> term an injury, is done them by the officers of the law
> they at once set about trying to secure some retalia-
> tion. On Saturday night Mr. Wade Plumley, who is
> a Constable for his brother, Magistrate J.D. Plumley
> was a member of a party which made a raid on the
> Dark Corner section and cut up several stills. The
> men whose stills were raided, chanced to know that
> Mr. Plumley was a member of the party and at once
> they determined that some revenge must be had upon
> him…Monday morning when Mr. Plumley went to
> his lot he found his fine cow lying on the ground in a
> puddle of blood. He made an examination of her and
> found that her throat had been cut, he then went on
> to his barn and found that his buggy had been torn in
> splinters…Of course there is no way of ascertaining
> who did the work, their names will probably never be**

**known. Acts similar to this have been committed by
the lawless in that section of the country many times
but not once have the perpetrators been caught and
punished for it. The work is done in the still hours
of the night and as there is no police protection in
that country the men have no trouble in keeping
their identity unknown…Policeman Rector was once
Magistrate for Highland Township and he has had
considerable dealings with moonshiners. "They never
did anything to me but I have known them to do
things that bordered on barbarism. When their anger
is stirred nothing is too low for them to do."[224]**

Operating in the void of the law and engaging in deeds that
delved into "barbarism" are strong words, but they had a ring of truth
to them. Wade Plumley made the mistake of cooperating with the
outsiders against members of his own community. In some circles,
Plumley was fortunate that the only thing killed on his farm was his
milking cow and not himself or a member of his family. Reports such
as these embodied the frustration of the boosters common during
this period. They hoped that if the illegal activity of the Dark Corner
could be suppressed, the county could remove the last anachronistic
element and promote itself as an idealized vision of the New South.[225]

By 1906, however, the growth of temperance had begun to
penetrate even the Dark Corner. Fed up with the constant violence
that had carried on intermittently for nearly forty years, some citizens
of the Dark Corner let their opinions be known with a public
statement made from Glassy Mountain Church:

**"Fair Warning. No more stills will be allowed within
four miles of this place. We mean business. Law adding citizens." This bold legend, placarded on the door
of the Glassy Mountain Church, in the very heart**

of Greenville County's Dark Corner, is the outward
sign of radical change of sentiment in that quarter…
Though Glassy Mountain's fair name has been spoiled
by many dark and bloody deeds and many years
of open defiance of the law, there have been in the
community all along men of different stripes. They
have endured with growing anger and impatience the
outrages of their turbulent neighbors, and now their
righteousness wrath have crystallized in a defiant,
organized movement to eradicate illicit distilling, the
cause of all their woes. They are nor running to the
revenue officers here, so far as may be learned, not
one of them has disclosed the location or ownership
of a single still. But they are serving notice on their
moonshining neighbors that they must shut up shop
and quit the business, or take the consequences…To
some one's suggestion that maybe members of the new
law and order movement might meet the fate that has
overtaken several revenue officers, the gentleman was
describing the change of sentiment and that enough
good and brave men were in the movement to make it
formidable. "If a single one of us is harmed for this"
he said, "we will rise up and clean the moonshiners
and rowdies out of our section just like you would
clean the rats out of a barn. If necessary we will shoot
them down like rattlesnakes." They have got to realize
that times have changed.[226]

The New South had spread to elements of the Dark Corner. New
South rhetoric was developing in the area, as some religious local
residents outside of the illicit distillation industry began to adhere
to what the boosters had been arguing for over two decades. While
these temperance-minded individuals opposed the long-standing
tradition of illegal distillation, a bit of the Dark Corner remained in
them. Though "temperate" on the alcohol issue they still encouraged

justice through some of the violent measures common in the liquor community. The notion that the pious citizens of the Dark Corner were just as willing to take up arms in defense of their lifestyle, as were the moonshiners in defense of their livelihood, is indeed telling. With the argument, "stop and obey the law, or I will kill you" it appears that these individuals had one foot in the New South and one foot still in their Dark Corner culture.[227]

The Beginning of the End

This internal effort did not stop illicit liquor production in the Dark Corner. It did, however, signal a new era. While the Dark Corner continued to supply liquor through the tenure of the Dispensary and State prohibition, the it had become more and more exposed to the outside world.[228] In particular, the large influx of outsiders during the First World War made lasting changes on the Dark Corner.[229]

During the First World War, Glassy Mountain Township was host to the range for the artillery training base of Camp Wadsworth, South Carolina.[230] Troops came up from the outskirts of Spartanburg City and fired live artillery into the side of Hogback Mountain.[231] As with most southerners who encountered troops in training during the First World War, the citizens of the Dark Corner were welcoming of the soldiers, even though it meant temporarily dropping their distrust of outsiders.[232] Part of the reason for this friendliness was that distillers made side profits off the soldiers camped around Glassy, and many others made money selling homemade foods and goods to the soldiers.[233]

After the War, the camp closed and the soldiers left, but the First World War had further exposed the Dark Corner to outsiders. Nonetheless, some in the community resumed their traditional

practices. The arrival of national prohibition in the 1920s, gave Dark
Corner distillers a larger market for their illicit alcohol.[234] Although
most of the South had been dry before the national initiative,
distillations made in the Dark Corner soon began to fill the demand
of those who were seeking relief from the new ban on alcohol.
However, with the introduction of outsiders into the Dark Corner
and the exodus of Dark Corner residence to other economic ventures
in the cities of the northeast; one newspaper editor was curious
enough to ponder whether these changes would have an effect on the
price of contraband whiskey.[235]

The end of national prohibition and the depression, however,
did not bring an end to illicit distillation in the Dark Corner.[236]
But, this double blow to the economy of the Dark Corner greatly
weakened the illicit activity in the area.[237] From 1935 onward, illicit
liquor activity dwindled, although there were a few notable flare ups
of activity. Throughout the 1950s, illegal, but modernized operations
that distilled via concentrated steam were raided in the Dark Corner
by local and Federal law enforcement.[238] The end of Dark Corner
distillation was not due to a massive demonstration of force by
Federal and State law enforcement. It was the result of a simple
$1.50 a gallon reduction in the liquor tax in 1964 and a falling profit
margin due to the price inflation of ingredients.[239]

The Revenue Wars in the Dark Corner had been a protracted
and bloody struggle. Over one hundred years after the introduction
of Revenue Law and the campaign of the New South Boosters, the
Dark Corner finally became quiet. Modernization crept into the
Dark Corner during the century following the rise of the Redeemer
government and finally brought an effective end to the wildness of the
area.[240] However, some of the elements present in the Dark Corner

through its wildest days still remained, or at least remained in the memories of its long-term inhabitants.

Chapter Four

The Darkness Evaporated: The Collective Memory of the Dark Corner

"There are some of the best people in that area"

While the industry blossomed throughout the Upstate in the twentieth century, the Dark Corner had remained isolated and impoverished. No longer a major producer of illicit liquor after the 1950s, many relocated to the various cotton mills. However, much of the character of the area remained intact through the middle of the century. After the Second World War, the cultural differences and criminal elements that were once common in the area began to become more of a curiosity than a constant reality. The Dark Corner became an area of interest to those nostalgic for the dying Appalachian culture as well as those who were intent on preserving the cultural elements that made the community unique.[241]

In the summer of 1983, Limestone College and the South Carolina Committee for the Humanities conducted a cultural study of the Dark Corner under the direction of Professor Bernard Zaidman. Knowing full well the traditional views of the Dark Corner and its violent notoriety, Zaidman and other historians went there with the intention of documenting the oral traditions of the few remaining natives. In a series of conversations with the elderly native born citizens and long term inhabitants, the committee produced an extensive cultural document that provided much insight into the rich culture of the Dark Corner and its clear ties to Appalachia.

While the Dark Corner was known for violence and illegal liquor in the nineteenth and early twentieth century, the community slowly changed as illegal distillation fell out of favor economically.[242] "The darkness had already evaporated a lot when I came to Gowansville," reminisced Fay Lanford in 1983, a former preacher in the Dark Corner; "But there are some of the best people in that area."[243] In that simple statement, Lanford echoed a common sentiment of the residents of the Dark Corner. The inhabitants believed that they were common and decent individuals. While most acknowledged the troubled history of the area, they were quick to dismiss the violence that was once prevalent as a fact of life in the Dark Corner.

One reoccurring theme that drove the conversations with the aging citizens was what had made, and continued to make, their area unique from the remainder of South Carolina. Many noted that the citizens of the Dark Corner had more important allegiances than those to governments and laws. Furthermore, the local concept of what constituted a native was tightly constricted by blood lines, geographic locale, and trust within the community.[244] Likewise, the definition of a "foreigner" was greatly expanded to even include those from the city of Greenville and neighboring communities.[245]

The citizens of the Dark Corner had been recognized as culturally unique from their counterparts in the other areas of Greenville and Spartanburg counties.[246] One notable characteristic separating the citizens of the Dark Corner from the remainder of South Carolinians was their personal allegiances. The inhabitants of the Dark Corner found solace in their trust in God, family, and land. In a conversation pertaining to the Dark Corner's traditional allegiance to these three staples, Bennie Lee Sinclair stated:

> **I would almost put land first. I have seen that God is. The family Bartons I've known have been old style Christians. God is very important, but the theory of the land; when my great-aunts took me back and showed me where they used to live, the bitterness they have for the day, when that land was sold. It was sold for a dollar an acre. It sold to a man in Greenville who still owns it. But just the general bitterness toward him. My Barton family was so thrilled when we got this land, but because this land is very near Barton land and at least within sight of a corner of Hogback, they just felt like we were righting an old wrong almost. Would you think land comes before God and family?**[247]

Continuing her emphasis on the importance of land to the residents of Dark Corner, Sinclair theorized that:

> **In other words, if you took a Barton man … And they had a choice of selling their land or giving up Christianity with the old-style with it, you can always come back in. Or leaving their wife or something, I think they chose the land. I really do.**[248]

The favoritism of land over God is fairly common in Appalachian cultures. While holding belief in God, many in Appalachia hold looser ties to the organized Christian community, than they do to the land they grew up on.[249] Myrtle Lindsey concurred with Bennie Lee Sinclair, that this Dark Corner trinity of God, family, and land was the cultural foundation of the community. However, in the spirit of Dark Corner independence she placed her own unique spin on the subject, "No, I say, instead of land and family, family and land. The Lord comes first. Of course … I'm glad I have this [land] here."[250]

When asked about the common belief in the Dark Corner to hold allegiances to God, family, and their land, Fay Lanford, added another element to the picture, patriotism. In Lanford's view, the citizens of the Dark Corner were true to their beliefs. If an industry such as illicit distillation was afforded them through their tradition, then that was all the justification they needed. No law was about to bring a forceful end to a long standing and inherited tradition:

> **That's right, patriotism. They were patriotic, you might think the other person who knew he was breaking the law, making whiskey and selling this thing, you might say, there was that patriotism. But as they looked at it, they didn't see that it was any more wrong for them to make that and sell it, than it was for somebody to go to an open licensed liquor store and buy it and sell it. And from my standpoint as far as either of those is concerned, I don't see no difference myself. They knew they were breaking what the law *says*, but in their sense, they didn't, in their way of looking at it, they didn't see that they were doing anything more wrong than those people who were dressed up on Main Street.**[251]

Events outside of the Corner had little effect on their livelihood. Their world lay in the coves along the North Carolina border and that is where their attention was focused. The land underfoot, the family that offered cooperative protection, and the belief in a just God tying the greater community together was all that the Dark Corner needed for the foundation of their rule of law. Allegiance to these three cultural icons, not to man-made institutions such as governments and laws, made the common law of the Dark Corner.

One resident expressed the love of land in the community when he starkly commented: "If you want to get somebody stirred up you just start takin' some of their land. You got problems."[252] This ethos squarely connects the communities in the Dark Corner with greater Appalachian culture.

Other aspects of their culture ingrained in the citizens of the Dark Corner that outsiders who came into the region without invite or a direct tie had to be watched. Following the 1866 introduction of the permanent revenue tax, the citizens had a new more organized menace to treat with; the Internal Revenue agent. This individual, without reason, merit, sense, or mercy was unleashed on the community by a larger collection of strangers in some far off city. As far as they were concerned, he only had one intention, the imposition of financial or physical harm on the inhabitants of the community.

By the time that many interviews and surveys of the region were complete, those who had originally confronted the revenuers and were the purest embodiment of Appalachian culture had long since died.[253] However, in the 1980s their descendents still harbored resentment and clung onto many of the attitudes common to their ancestors. One account by Junior Pitman, a local magistrate in the Dark Corner, told of a wayfaring stranger who happened through the wrong community. Remembering the incident, "my mother and father, said one time there was a man walking just through the community and they came, several men came to the house and got him and laid him away. Said he'd insulted a woman or something and nobody never did hear what happened to him."[254]

The angst that surrounded the image of the stranger was not confined solely to those who were outsiders to the community. Other families in the Dark Corner were cause for concern. Ella Plumley remembered something that her father told her when she was young:

Me and my sister used to cow hunt, you know, we always just turn our cows out lose … And we'd always have to get the cows up in the afternoon, and Daddy always told us that what we seen, to keep it to ourself. And we did. That was none of our business, and it was none of his business, and it was not of nobody's business, what we saw, to keep it to ourself, and we did. Well, I saw a lot of 'em and I've been in 'em.[illicit liquor operations][255]

With the knowledge that many unscrupulous individuals in the community made a side living as informants, maintaining security was of the essence.[256] Perhaps his daughters were instructed to remain quiet due to the fact that children, in their truthful nature, could be easily enticed to reveal the illicit activities in the community and therefore become a liability to the family. Some of the most violent reactions in the Dark Corner came from those cut by revenuers after an informant's tip.[257] Even worse, was the knowledge that the operation had been destroyed because of the careless tongue of one's own blood.[258]

However, the Dark Corner was not always prejudiced towards outsiders. With the arrival of the artillery range on Hogback Mountain, some local residents had an opportunity to profit from the encampment. Remembering his father, a local store owner during the War, Alex Campbell reminisced about his experiences during the Army's stay around the Dark Corner:

He hauled the stuff from Campobello in a two-horse wagon, you know. Kept the soldiers in candy and cigarettes and stuff, and all kinds of drinks. Oh, ah, it would look like Christmas sometimes when we were going to school, you know. We look up there com-

ing back and see a streak of fire go over and hit the side of Hogback, a big old streak of fire, and see the smoke blooming up, and we'd get scared and say it come time the world coming to an end … I remember hearing my mother ask one of the captains, she cooked sometimes for the soldiers, and when the first gun was fired, I remember hearing her asking, "Is all that all the louder it's going to be?" You know, we just thought it was going to blow us out of the house.[259]

While the Campbells were accepting of the soldier's tenure in the Dark Corner, others were apprehensive. As the Army began to relocate families off of Hogback Mountain, some steadfastly refused to go. While talking about Morris Plumley, one of the few mountaineers that remained on the Mountain after the Army moved in, Campbell reminisced that:

He said it he come back, "I wouldn't have nothing." He said, "My house would be tore up and gone, burnt down and I ain't leaving it here." He stayed too. Old Dr. Moore tried to get him to leave too. She had a little young brother then, just a small child, and the doc told, it got sick. Doc said, "There ain't a thing in the world wrong with that child but shell shock. You better move out from there," he said. "All the young'uns are liable to die." No he didn't believe in that and he wouldn't move. But the child did die and the Doc said that was the trouble.[260]

The fact that a man was willing to risk the lives of his offspring for the possession of land he saw as his own is indeed telling of the culture in the Dark Corner. While the love of land is not in anyway unique to the Dark Corner, many of these individuals were set to maintain what was rightfully theirs, even in the face of extreme hazards. The thought of being pushed off the land by strangers was one of the greatest insults to be thrust upon them.[261]

"It wasn't too awful bad, somebody get killed every once in a while"

The distillation culture of the Dark Corner was the primary reason behind the lawlessness and violence that gained so much notoriety after the Civil War. As a seasonal supplement for a subsistence economy, it must be understood that not a single distiller was making an exorbitant profit.[262] The resources generated were not used to fund a lavish life style. Instead they were used to make ends meet and provide a little security that would not be found otherwise. The community accepted it because most of them were connected to the industry in some form.[263]

Alternatively, some inhabitants were willing participants through fear and extortion. The threat of a burning or an ambush was very real to those who crossed the illicit distillers and the community.[264] Whatever the reasoning, the results were real; the community was well connected to the illicit industry.[265] The question remains, how did the community view the industry? Some insight can be offered by how the grandchildren of many of the original nineteenth century moonshiners view the world according to whiskey.

Twenty-four of the thirty residents of the Dark Corner interviewed by Bernard Zaidman in the summer of 1983 had some story pertaining to illicit whiskey. The subject was rather matter of fact to the community. Whether through practice or nostalgia, the citizens of the Dark Corner had easily accepted the notion that their community was renowned for its distillation history.[266] The responses of the community were generally in agreement. The production of whiskey may be against the law, but it was certainly not a crime. In a sense, the illicit distillation economy of the Dark Corner became a community tie that was, by some, cherished with the pride of distinction. [267]

Death and murder in the Dark Corner were in most cases directly related to the illicit whiskey industry. The tone of many older inhabitants interviewed suggests that the slaying of a man was a natural event, particularly if it was related to liquor. Alex Campbell remembered another incident in which his father killed a drunken man who had besieged a gambling shack and was taking shots at everyone who fled:

> **Well. It wasn't too awful bad. Somebody get killed every once in a while. My dad killed a man. Man named Jim Sanders, lived in a house down there gamblin' down near Spartanburg County ... Says (his father), "Mr Sanders, what's the matter?" He says, "I'm gonna kill every son-of-a-bitch that comes out that front-door." My daddy had a 32 on him ... He just pulled his gun out in his hand and this fella standing there and ... he pointed it at the door, and my daddy says, "Well, I'm a-coming out. You better back out. ... I'd just as soon blow your head off as the next man's." ... and he said he seen his gun come on his hatband ... and my daddy heered his gun un'click though. Says, "He'd a-killed me first," but said he was gripped his hand up a little to furr and his hammer come back until it come back enough to hit his thumb before it made the last click to fall and my daddy's went off quicker than that.**[268]

This starkly nonchalant perception of death was widely held in the community. The fact the Campbell stated that the killing of a man, "wasn't too awful bad" demonstrates the area's acceptance

of violent death. The violence and death that coincided with the
liquor industry had become culturally accepted over the years. This
Dark Corner norm was substantially different from the mores of
the remainder of South Carolina. Contemplating this story and its
connection to the conversation, Campbell remarked that:

> **Yeah, you find a man like that now and then. They get
> to fighting over some whiskey. Most of the people I
> ever knowed of up in there that, got killed, they got
> killed over whiskey. Fighting 'cause they was point-
> ing on another's still or something or other ... and he
> says, "I'm gonna kill you for it," and all like that. All I
> could hear when I was a young boy growing up.[269]**

The whiskey business and death seemed to go hand in hand.
Many understood that if you dabbled in the whiskey operation, there
was a distinct chance that you would have to kill or be killed.[270] The
community accepted this because it was a manifestation of their
independent culture. In their minds it is a God given right to use
their land for any purpose they saw fit to provide for their family. The
outsiders, the government and informants, had no right to intervene
in their livelihood and they should be left to their own free will.

The resulting mentality of the community was that the crimes
being committed were not crimes, but defense of natural rights
being infringed upon by outsiders.[271] This was a classic image of
what most perceived as American independence. With such a deep-
rooted tradition that centers on the control of their own destiny;
"crimes" such as illicit distillation become acceptable.[272] Side effects,
such as murder and increased pressure by law enforcement, were just
bothersome conditions that came as a result of their culture.

Folk in the Dark Corner came to accept one aspect of the moonshine economy they did not like, the revenue agent. Randy Emory expressed his sentiments about the precarious condition of the moonshine community to Zaidman:

> **When you worked, the bad thing about moonshining is you were making good money too, couldn't spend any 'cause then everybody knew you were making it ... So, and then it get gone, it'd seem like that money didn't go that far, but when I was little, it never failed, every time Daddy bought a car, if it was a fairly late model car, the revenuers would walk that creek back to the house, up and down, for two weeks, they'd walk that creek to find out if he has a still place.[273]**

The "corruption" of the informant system and the revenuer agent became legendary in the Dark Corner. According to local tradition, revenue agents were allowed to bring sparse evidence into the courtroom and gain convictions from it. The informants' testimonies were taken as the gospel and those who had a vendetta against certain members of the community were sometimes able to abuse their position to remove their rivals.[274] Randy Emory remembers a story that his father told him about a local informant and the demise of an innocent man by the name of Elliot Pittman:

> **Well, one of the revenuers swore to this man's track and he got time out of it. They never caught the man, I don't think they ever saw him, but back then in the old killing thing, Jim Howard's daddy, well he was killed, and Elliot Pittman and his sons were accused of killing him. And they got Wade Plumley, my grand uncle, to swear Elliot Pittman's track and he did, and he did not see Elliot Pittman make that track.[275]**

Directing his disgust at the informant system as well as the informant, he continued:

> **Now that to me, I don't know how any man could swear to a track that he didn't see a man make, but for goodness sakes, somebody could have been wearing that man's shoes, you know! But he did, Wade Plumely swore Elliot Pitman's track and I mean that's part of the old song, the old ballad.**[276]

The negative image of the revenuer had become so developed in the Dark Corner by the turn of the twentieth century "he" began to appear in local ballads. Ballads were a common and often personal way of recording events in Appalachia and expressed the emotion surrounding notorious events.[277] Reciting the ballad, Emory sang: "Ruben Gosnell, took Pittman to jail, says, 'I'll be coming back'; he came back and got Wade Plumley, to swear to Elliot's track." Commenting on the ballad, Emory noted:

> **And I used to sing it, "He came back and got Wade Plumley, (that sorry grand uncle of mine) to swear to Elliot's track." I would always stop and interject that because I, even as a child, that bothered me that he would swear to a track that he didn't see a man make. I just found it ingracious that he'd do that.**[278]

In the minds of many native residents of the Dark Corner, the informant system was the worst characteristic of the revenuer "invasion." The revenuer informant was an individual who embodied the most negative attributes. This man made a profit by trespassing on others' property, looking for the signs of illicit distillation that might net the small informant's fee.[279] While in many cases informants were individuals who had a family grudge against the producer or were in some cases a rival producer, the negative connotation of being an informant was a stigma that individuals did not desire to shoulder, as there were obvious consequences such as retaliation and murder.[280]

None the less, despite the stigma, there were those who still chose to be informants. Randy Emory described the informant network in the Dark Corner as one based on advantageous revenge:

> **A lot of reporting, some people were, well you always have religious fanatics, and they thought it was a big crime for some people here, and then family feuding, somebody get mad at somebody else, I'll turn him in, and they get mad and say, I think he turned me in, I think I'll turn him in. So it got back like that.[281]**

Much like the warning placed on the door of Glassy Mountain Church in 1906, the distilling community had to be mindful of those who had religious motivations for turning informant. The anti-drink platform of denominations such as the Baptists, caused headaches for distillers who had to contend with the "saved" flock. However, at times those motivated with the spirit of the Lord overstepped their boundaries when lashing out against illegal liquor. One famous account came from Alvin Howard who remembered hearing a story from his father about a local church storing ammunition in a backroom in anticipation of possible trouble. In a spectacle befitting of the Dark Corner, the church caught fire and blew up.[282] The actions of these "religious fanatics" were looked down upon by many in the Dark Corner who believed in God, but stayed independent of organized religion.[283]

Another side effect from the fear of the informant system was "wildcatting." Traditionally, wildcatting was described as those who entered the industry with the express notion of making a quick run, usually of poorer quality, then exiting the distillation business with a quick profit.[284] Wildcatting had been traditionally frowned upon by those who made a living off seasonal liquor and the practice generally had a negative connotation as it tended to occur in times of high market demand.[285]

However, one type of wildcatter often overlooked is those who "put on." Wildcatters who "put on" usually approached an established still operator and demanded access to his still for their personal use, in exchange for their silence. Former Dark Corner moonshiner Randy Emory, outlined an experience with a wildcatter in his younger days:

> **Back then if you had a still place, it cost you to set a place up. I mean it's not like somebody thinks you go out and put you a few barrels, they have to make their borders, and their tubeings and their pipes and everything. And somebody that couldn't afford it, he'd walk around and he'd find the still place and he'd just add him a few barrels on. He wouldn't have all the initial expense. And what could you do? You had to finish your run out, if you told him he couldn't put on, he'd have you turned in so you were between a rock and a hard place. Most of the time they'd finish their run out and he'd get one good run out of it and it wouldn't cost him anything.[286]**

The notion of the moonshiner is well established in the Dark Corner. The mythic image once held by outsiders was of an area full of drunken "hillbillies" aimlessly shooting one another over their product.[287] However, illicit distillation was one of the cultural cornerstones of the community. The image of liquor production, and even mild responsible consumption, was a positive one within the Dark Corner.[288] While nostalgia brought many positive reminiscences about liquor over the years and the image of the moonshiners has been romanticized in their minds, there was certainly a dark side to a community that focused its economy largely around illegal liquor production.[289] In reminiscing about tales his father had told him, Pink Campbell remembered the fate of one particular family:

> **There was a family moved in over yonder 'round Glassy and a bunch of people went in there and just killed 'em and burned the house and them up too, afraid the'd tell on 'em about the whiskey business, you know, and they just killed 'em and burnt 'em up.[290]**

When the extremely violent side of the community reared its ugly head, the results were often dire. The price for this particular family's loose tongue, or open eyes, was the loss of life and property at the hands of a murderous mob.[291] Events like this one were not isolated. Another noted burning involved the local school, a teacher fond of corporal punishment, and a disgruntled moonshiner.

The story holds that in the 1920s a new teacher at the school, Miles Hutchinson, was confronted with some large and bothersome students. Taking the situation into hand, he lined up the boys and gave them lashings with a hickory switch. The boys naturally told their fathers that evening and a confrontation was brewing for the next day. The next morning before the onset of the school day, a group of fathers arrived at the school and called Mr. Hutchinson out. One father was rather flamboyant about the situation and beckoned the teacher to come over to attempt at beating him. Lunging from the top steps into the crowd of disgruntled fathers, the teacher did just that, as the rest stood back stunned. According to Thomas D. West, that evening the school was set afire with the school teacher and his wife inside, upstairs sleeping in the loft. They managed to make it out by fashioning a rope out of bed sheets. The result was an expensive and costly lesson on family loyalty in the Dark Corner, as the "foreign" teacher lost all that he had in the fire.[292]

Violent community flare-ups and tragic events were not the only hazards of the Dark Corner. Exciting events such as burnings only occurred once in a great while. In daily life, it was a burdensome task to navigate around the unsavory characters of the community. Pink Campbell described one such man. He remembered one individual from his youth who gave constant quarrel to his father and the community, Early Harrison. Campbell remarked:

> **They said Early Harrison's the one that shot that man. He killed a man over there. This man stole his liquor and went to sell it, was selling it to a man over in Green's Creek and he killed the man from Green's Creek ... I used to know Early, and I was over at his house, and he'd been huntin' and he come in with a gun on his shoulder and he said he'd found a patch of corn over there and he was going back. It was late in the Spring and they hadn't gathered it. He thought it ought to be his. I never said a word to him. [about claiming the corn as his own] He might have shot me. Not like somebody was arguing with him, was it? ... Old man Bill said he was the meanest man ever was around in there.**[293]

The culture of the Dark Corner, however, did not entirely revolve around the illicit distillation industry and its resulting violence. There were other more peaceful pursuits. Farming and logging, for example, were common.[294] The citizens of the Dark Corner, like most southerners in rural poverty, were hard workers. A few led successful commercial ventures and had no need to undertake illicit production.[295] For the farmers, their agrarian occupations came first and the illicit industry was the boost that helped them make it through the year economically. As with many areas in Appalachia, employment in the lumber industry could be an alternative to moonshining, as popular as the illegal industry was.[296] One timber worker reminisced:

> **I guess the livelihood of most people in this area woulda been moonshining and cutting locust posts and a little bit of corn raising. Back before my time and in my younger years and we didn't think of it as being wrong or bad. A little moonshining in that day and time, it's just illegal as far as tax purposes ... As far back as I can remember there's been some saw milling in this area and locust posts and I can remember the day when usually your weekly groceries came from going out on your property and cuttin' some locust posts and trading 'em. They didn't wanta buy them and pay money ... I believe it was called [referring to barter] ... and buy you whatever the general store had with that. You didn't need to have money to get then.[297]**

Small scale woodcutting fit well into the Appalachian economy of the Dark Corner that still had barter elements in it. Foodstuffs, cottage production, lumber, and liquor were all acceptable currencies in the Dark Corner. However, only whiskey brought the hard currency offered by outsiders.[298]

The differences that Appalachian culture brought the Dark Corner resulted in contempt of the area by nineteenth century boosters and belated fascination by anthropologists in the twentieth century. Many contemporary accounts throughout the nineteenth century, and early portions of the twentieth century, comment on how unique the inhabitants of the Dark Corner were. The community had drawn notoriety from outsiders as being a place full of poor moonshining hillbillies who were not to be trusted. Often when a citizen of the Dark Corner ventured into larger communities outside his homeland, his presence was greeted with hostility. Alex Campbell recounts a story of one individual that was practicing an avocation that was an alternative to moonshining and the hostility he encountered in Greenville:

> **Massy Howard, he had an old mule and sled. He'd get up in them mountains there and get all kinds of shrubbery. Get old laurels and ivys ad haul 'em to Greenville and sell 'em. That's the way he made his living. He wasn't fooling with no whiskey back then. … Got a good price for 'em. People thought they come from the nursery. They finally got him up one day and some fella scared him up around Greenville, one of the deputy sheriffs or somebody got him and they run him out, told him, "Why you going up on the mountains and getting them little old wildflowers and bring 'em down and sell these people at a big price? Why, we gonna put you in jail." It scared him to death. He quit carrying 'em; he come back home. Says, If you gonna sell something down there, you gotta recommend what it is, you can't go up there and dig it up in the mountains, an' fool these people up.[299]**

The residents of the Dark Corner faced many prejudices when they left their isolated coves. The outside world, just thirty odd miles away, was a place that frowned on their culture and mannerisms. The larger communities had their own cultural ethics that did not largely mesh with those found in the Dark Corner. According to many outsider opinions, throughout the nineteenth and early twentieth centuries, the coves of the Dark Corner were abundant with uneducated rustics who made their living by producing illegal intoxicants.[300] In the end, the South Carolina of the twenty-first century has no place for the rural mountain values and illicit distillation that gave the Dark Corner its colorful past.

Conclusion

Pristine Mountain Living: The Death of the Dark Corner

The Dark Corner's history was tumultuous. Dangerous settlement in the Appalachian frontier, the hazards of the American Revolution, political isolation during the antebellum period, dissent during the Civil War, and a protracted struggle with revenue enforcement had a lasting effect on the area's mentality.[301] Coupled with a strong and dominant current of Appalachian culture in the area, the Dark Corner brought to South Carolina a cultural anomaly that is often associated more with western North Carolina and eastern Kentucky than with South Carolina itself.

The Appalachian culture that developed in the area clearly differentiated from other portions of the state. The Appalachian culture, with its reliance on distillation and mistrust of outsiders created an environment that was hostile to development. This reliance on an alcohol economy kept it ostracized by those who attempted to better the Upstate and left the Dark Corner largely out of the New South.[302]

According to outsiders, illicit liquor related lawlessness was the most negative trait found in the Dark Corner. While many factors contributed to the development of lawlessness, nothing did more to exacerbate it than the mishandling of the Revenue Act in the Dark Corner. The Federal government's continued efforts to suppress illicit distillation in the area and the implementation of harsh tactics ultimately made matters much worse. For over one hundred years, the agencies that evolved into the modern Internal Revenue Service spent a lot of resources trying to quell illicit activity in the Dark Corner. In the end, none of those charged with combating resistance to the excise taxes correctly identified the root of the problem. While the various agencies in Washington were content to relegate the problem to mere tax delinquency and viewed resistance as the desperate act of outlaws, they were oblivious to the cultural and economic context of the struggle.[303]

Essentially, the failure of the Untied States to acknowledge the cultural and economic factors behind home distillation was the root cause of the most violent resistance. After outlawing the practice, the Federal government failed to present the whiskey-producing population with a viable economic alternative. In the minds of the inhabitants, the illegalization of a cultural activity older than its enforcing government was on par with outright persecution.[304] Thus, the issue went beyond liquor. The government's error in viewing the illicit activity of the Dark Corner as a legal issue, not a cultural conflict, and pursuing it accordingly, exacerbated the struggle. While the 1878 offer of clemency temporarily bridged the cultural gap, by demonstrating some form of understanding, ultimately the United States never effectively addressed the questions of tradition.[305]

The ultimate death knell for the Appalachian distillation culture, however, had its roots in the economy. Following the reduction of the excise tax in the 1960s, illicit distillation became unprofitable. With many of the home distillers' impoverished clientele making the switch to bonded liquor, the distillers were simply forced into other lines of work. Accelerating this trend was an inflationary rise in prices and a reduction in the profit margin garnered by illicit distillation. This resulted in the functional death of home distillation as an industry. The practice of home distillation became a fascinating novelty that was relegated to those who whished to produce for private consumption.[306]

While the illicit distillation industry has since died in the Dark Corner, the cunning and enterprising spirit of underground activity lives on. Local residents have noted that marijuana cultivation began to develop in the Dark Corner around the same time illicit distilling fell from fashion.[307] The growth of marijuana, and the later production of crystal methamphetamine, both stand as perverse monuments to the remnants of Appalachian independence. The popularity and profit margin found in these late twentieth century developments, provides merit to the argument that many of the inhabitants of rural Appalachia were opting for that "easy out" through "wildcatting."[308]

The attempts of the New South boosters to paint the Dark Corner as a bastion of backwardness only maintained the rift between the modernized sections of South Carolina and the Dark Corner. The projection of negative stereotypes on the Dark Corner continued its isolation as it became largely associated with lawlessness to the outside world through the New South editors.[309] In the end, the New South campaigners hurt the Dark Corner. They did not bring about the sobriety they so desperately sought; instead they permanently branded the Dark Corner as a negative anomaly that was to be looked at with wonder, and to be largely segmented from regional modernization.[310]

The eventual modernization of the surrounding area, however, did much to bring an end to Appalachian culture in the Dark Corner. As the Upstate continued to modernize in the latter part of the twentieth century, and the need for labor grew even further, the Dark Corner began to open to the idea of employment outside the region.[311]

In the end, no matter how the inhabitants of the Dark Corner resisted modernization, their efforts were futile. As Greenville grew, the borderlands between the Dark Corner and modernized South Carolina shrank.[312] As Greenville emerged as an economic leader in the State in the 1980s, the Dark Corner was vicariously opened through proximity. However, it was only a matter of time before the isolation came to an end.[313] By the late 1980s the distinct Appalachian distillation culture of the Dark Corner was all but a recent memory. The remaining natives of Hogback and Glassy Mountains had vacated their coves. It was not due to a massive government crackdown on illicit distillation, or a result of another wave of eminent domain by the United States government. The Dark Corner fell to a widening trend in the American South, resort development.[314]

Starting in 1989, the Dark Corner became host to a series of developments that transformed the area overnight. As golf course development took over some of the more prominent landscapes of the area, the Dark Corner began a new chapter in its history of isolation; the gated community. This breach of the Dark Corner's rural isolation was catastrophic to the fragile remnants of the culture that remained.[315]

Now, the Appalachian culture once present in South Carolina can only be found in the reminiscences of the elderly. Modernization, economic opportunities, wars, education, internal improvements, immigration, and gentrification have all shone light into the Dark Corner. For better or worse, the northwestern portions of South Carolina are now some of the most progressive and accommodating areas of the State. The modern attitude of the mountains is a complete reversal from what was common only a century ago.[316]

Within the Dark Corner, as with many of the coves throughout Appalachia, isolation was swiftly replaced by open courting of ecotourism and resort development.[317] Once known for its foreboding wilderness, the Dark Corner is now known for its scenic beauty as the "Golden Corner" of South Carolina. Once notorious for its backwardness and poverty, now many of the most progressive individuals in the Upstate live in some of the more expensive real estate in South Carolina. The couple dozen miles that separated the City of Greenville from the Dark Corner has now dwindled to an acceptable morning commute.[318]

Culture, not specifically the distillation of whiskey, created the Dark Corner, in mind and myth. However, the death of Appalachian culture in South Carolina was inevitable.[319] Since there was never a large concentration of those affected by the cultural mores, it was slowly taken over by the outsiders who moved into the area. The extinction of Appalachian culture in South Carolina was a loss for the rich cultural diversity of the State; it became the victim of the "glorious" modernization touted today throughout the Upstate.[320]

SELECTED BIBLIOGRAPHY

PUBLIC DOCUMENTS AND PRINTED COLLECTIONS

Davis v. South Carolina, 107 U. S. 597 (1883)

Tales From the Dark Corner: Documenting the Oral Tradition.
Greenville, South Carolina: Greenville Public Library.

Letters Received by the Department of South Carolina, 1871-1884.
Microfilm. National Archives and Records Administration,
Washington D.C.

BOOKS

Abramson, Rudy and Jean Haskell. eds. *Encyclopedia of Appalachia*.
Knoxville: University of Tennessee Press, 2006.

Adams, Shelby Lee. *Appalachian Legacy: Photographs*. Jackson:
University of Mississippi Press, 1998.

--------. *Appalachian Lives*. Jackson: University of Mississippi Press,
2003.

--------. *Appalachian Portraits*. Jackson: University of Mississippi Press, 1993.

Allison, Thomas R. *Moonshine Memories*. Montgomery, Alabama: New South Books, 2001.

Alston, Lee J. and Joseph P. Ferrie. *Southern Paternalism and the American Welfare State: Economics, Politics, and Institutions in the South, 1865-1965. New York: Cambridge University Press, 1999.*

Ayers, Edward. *Vengeance and Justice: Crime and Punishment in the 19th Century American South.* New York: Oxford University Press, 1984.

Batson, Mann. *The Upper Part of Greenville County, South Carolina.* Taylors, SC: Faith Printing Company, 1993

Becker, Jane S. *Selling Tradition : Appalachia and the Construction of an American folk, 1930-1940.* Chapel Hill: University of North Carolina Press, 1998.

Behr, Edward. *Prohibition: Thirteen Years that Changed America.* New York: Arcade Publishing, 1996.

Belcher, Ray, *Greenville County, South Carolina: From Cotton Fields to Textile Center of the World.* Charleston, SC: History Press, 2006.

Blethen, H. Tyler and Curtis W. Wood Jr. ed. *Ulster and North America: Transatlantic Perspectives on the Scotch-Irish.* Tuscaloosa: University of Alabama Press, 1997.

Burts, Robert Milton. *Richard Irvine Manning and the Progressive Movement in South Carolina*. Columbia: University of South Carolina Press, 1974.

Bynum, Victoria E. *The Free State of Jones: Mississippi's Longest Civil War*. Chapel Hill: University of North Carolina Press, 2001.

Campbell , John C. *The Southern Highlander and His Homeland*. Lexington: University of Kentucky Press, 1969.

Carlton, David L. *Mill and Town in South Carolina: 1880-1920*. Baton Rouge: Louisiana State University Press, 1982.

Carr, Jess. *The Second Oldest Profession: An Informal History of Moonshining in America*. Englewood Cliffs, New Jersey: Prentice-Hall, 1972.

Carson, Gerald. *The Social History of Bourbon: An Unhurried Account of Our Star-Spangled American Drink*. New York: Dodd, Mead, 1963.

Coffin, Tristram. *The British Traditional Ballad in North America*. Philadelphia: American Folklore Society, 1963.

Coker, Joe L. *Liquor in the Land of the Lost Cause: Southern White Evangelicals and the Prohibition Movement. Lexington: University of Kentucky Press, 200)*.

Cooper, William J. *The Conservative Regime: South Carolina, 1877-1890*. Baltimore: John Hopkins University Press, 1968.

Coulter, E. Merton. *The South During Reconstruction, 1865-1877.* Baton Rouge: Louisiana State University Press, 1947.

Crain, J. Dean. *A Mountain Boy's Life Story.* Greenville, SC: Baptist Courier, 1914.

Current, Richard Nelson. *Lincoln's Loyalist: Union Soldiers from the Confederacy.* Lebanon, New Hampshire: University Press of New England, 1992.

Dabney, Joseph Earl. *Mountain Spirits: A Chronicle of Corn Whiskey From King James' Ulster Plantation to America's Appalachians and the Moonshine Life.* Asheville, North Carolina: Bright Mountain Books, 1974.

--------. *More Mountain Sprits: The Continuing Chronicle of Moonshine Life and Corn Whiskey, Wines, Ciders &Beers in America's Appalachians.* Asheville, North Carolina: Bright Mountain Books, 1980.

Drago, Edmund L. *Hurrah For Hampton: Black Red Shirts in South Carolina During Reconstruction.* Fayetteville: University of Arkansas Press, 1998.

Drake, Richard B. *A History of Appalachia.* Lexington: University of Kentucky Press, 2001.

Downard, William L. *Dictionary of the History of the American Brewing and Distilling Industries*. Westport Connecticut: Greenwood Press, 1980.

Dunn, Durwood. *Cades Cove: The Life and Death of a Southern Appalachian Community, 1818-1937*. Knoxville: University of Tennessee Press, 1988.

Edgar, Walter. *South Carolina: A History*. Columbia: University of South Carolina Press, 1998.

Edgar, Walter. ed., *The South Carolina Encyclopedia. Columbia: University of South Carolina Press, 2006.*

Ellison, Betty Boles. *Illegal Odyssey: 200 Years of Kentucky Moonshine*. Self-Published: Betty Boles Ellison, 2003.

Foner, Eric. *America's Reconstruction: People and Politics After the Civil War*. Baton Rouge: Louisiana State University Press, 1997.

Ford, Lacy K. *Origins of Southern Radicalism: The South Carolina Upcountry, 1800-1860*. Oxford: Oxford University Press, 1988.

Franklin, John Hope. *The Militant South*. Cambridge: Belknap Press of Harvard University, 1956.

Freehling, William W. *Prelude to Civil War: The Nullification Controversy in South Carolina, 1816-1836*. New York: Oxford University Press, 1965.

--------. *The South vs. The South: How Anti-Confederate Southerners Shaped the Course of the Civil War.* New York: Oxford University Press, 2001.

Gaston, Paul M. *The New South Creed: A Study in Southern Mythmaking.* Baton Rouge: Louisiana State University Press, 1976.

Gregory, James V. and James Walton Lawrence Sr.. *Indians, Bloodshed, Tears, Churches, & Schools: It all Started at Fort Gowan.* Landrum, South Carolina: Lawrence, 2003.

Hendricks, Anne H. *The Dark Corner of Greenville* County. Edited By Jeffry R. Willis. Greenville: The Greenville County Historical Society, 1998.

Hogeland, William. *The Whiskey Rebellion: George Washington, Alexander Hamilton, and the Frontier Rebels who Challenged America's Newfound Sovereignty.* New York: Scribner, 2006.

Howard, James A. *Dark Corner Heritage.* Self Published, 1980.

Howe, Frederic C. *Taxation and Taxes in the United States under the Internal Revenue System, 1791-1895.* New York: T. Y. Crowell, 1896.

Hu, Tun Yuan. *The Liquor Tax in the United States, 1791-1947: A History of the Internal Revenue Taxes Imposed on Distilled Spirits by the Federal Government.* New York: Graduate School of Business, Columbia University, 1950.

Huff ,Archie Vernon Jr. *Greenville: The History of the City and County in the South Carolina Piedmont*. Columbia: University of South Carolina Press, 1995.

Huggins, Phillip Kenneth. *The South Carolina Dispensary: a Bottle Collector's Atlas and History of the System*. Columbia: Sandlapper Press, 1971.

Hughes, Jerry. *Once Upon a Time in Pickens County: The Amos Ladd and Lewis R. Redmond Story*. Self Published, 1993.

Inscoe, John C. & Gordon B. McKinney. *The Heart of Confederate Appalachia: Western North Carolina in the Civil War*. Chapel Hill: The University of North Carolina Press, 2000.

Inscoe, John C. and Robert C. Kenzer, eds. *Enemies of the Country: New Perspectives on Unionist in the Civil War South*. Athens: University of Georgia Press, 2001.

Kantrowitz, Stephen. *Ben Tillman & the Reconstruction of White Supremacy*. Chapel Hill: University of North Carolina Press, 2000.

Kellner, Esther, *Moonshine: Its History and Folklore*. New York: Weathervane Books, 1971.

Kephart, Horace. *Our Southern Highlanders: a Narrative of Adventure in the Southern Appalachians and a Study of Life Among the Mountaineers*. Knoxville: University of Tennessee Press, 1984.

Kibler, Lillian Adele *Benjamin F. Perry: South Carolina Unionist.* Durham: Duke University Press, 1946.

Kirby, Jack Temple. *Rural Lost Worlds: The American South, 1920-1960.* Baton Rouge: Louisiana State University Press, 1987.

Kyvig, David E. *Repealing Prohibition.* Kent, Ohio: Kent State University Press, 2000.

Lawrence, James Walton Sr. *Hogback Country.* Landrum, SC: News Leader, 1982.

--------. *The Shadows of Hogback.* Landrum, SC: The News Leader, 1979.

--------. *Smokin' Shootin' Irons In Dark Corner.* Landrum, South Carolina: Lawrence, 2000.

Malone, Bill C. *Singing Cowboys and Musical Mountaineers: Southern Culture and the Roots of Country Music.* Athens: University of Georgia Press, 2003.

Maurer, David W. *Kentucky Moonshine.* Lexington: University of Kentucky Press, 1974.

McCurry, Stephanie. *Masters of Small Worlds: Yeoman Households, Gender Relations, and the Political Culture of the Antebellum South Carolina Low Country.* New York: Oxford University Press, 1997.

McNeil, W.K. ed., *Appalachian Images in Folk and Popular Culture*. Knoxville, University of Tennessee Press, 1995.

Miller, Wilbur R. *Revenuers & Moonshiners: Enforcing Federal Liquor Law in the Mountain South, 1865-1900*. Chapel Hill: University of North Carolina Press, 1991.

Montgomery, Michael. *The Dictionary of Smoky Mountain English*. Knoxville: University of Tennessee Press, 2004.

--------. *From Ulster to America: The Scotch-Irish Heritage of American English*. Belfast: Ulster Historical Foundation, 2004.

Montgomery, Michael and Ellen Johnson, eds. *The New Encyclopedia of Southern Culture: Language*. Chapel Hill: University of North Carolina Press, 2007.

Murchison, Kenneth M. *Federal Criminal Law Doctrines: the Forgotten Influence of National Prohibition*. Durham, North Carolina: Duke University Press, 1994.

Poole, William Scott *Never Surrender: Confederate Memory and Conservation in the South Carolina Upcountry*. Athens: University of Georgia Press, 2004.

Pudup, Mary Beth. Dwight B. Billings, Altina L. Waller, ed., *Appalachia in the Making: the Mountain South in the Nineteenth Century*. Chapel Hill: University of North Carolina Press, 1995.

Rabinowitz, Howard N. *The First New South, 1865-1920*. Arlington Heights, Illinois: Harlan Davidson, 1992.

Rehder, John B. *Appalachian Folkways*. Baltimore: John Hopkins University Press, 2004.

Rorabaugh, W. J. *The Alcoholic Republic: An American Tradition*. New York: Oxford University Press, 1979.

Rumbarger, John J. *Power, Profits, and Prohibition: Alcohol Reform and the Industrialization of America, 1800-1930*. Albany: State University of New York Press, 1989.

Scally, Robert James. *The End of Hidden Ireland: Rebellion, Famine, & Emigration*. New York: Oxford University Press, 1995.

Schmeckebier, Laurence F. and Francis X. Eble. *The Bureau of Internal Revenue: Its History, Activities and Organization*. Baltimore: John Hopkins University Press, 1923.

Shapiro, Henry D. *Appalachia on Our Mind: the Southern Mountains and Mountaineers in American Consciousness, 1870-1920*. Chapel Hill: University of North Carolina Press, 1978.

Sinclair, Andrew. *Prohibition: The Era of Excess*. Boston: Little & Brown, 1962.

Tindall, George B. *The Emergence of the New South, 1913-1945*. Baton Rouge: Louisiana State University Press, 1967.

Tullos, Allen. *Habits of Industry: White Culture and the Transformation of the Carolina Piedmont.* Chapel Hill: University of North Carolina Press, 1989.

Weller, Jack E. *Yesterday's People: Life in Contemporary Appalachia.* Lexington: University of Kentucky Press, 1965.

Williams , Cratis D., *Southern Mountain Speech.* Berea, Kentucky: Berea College Press, 1992.

Williams, John Alexander. *Appalachia: A History.* Chapel Hill: University of North Carolina Press, 2002.

Williamson, Joel. *After Slavery: the Negro in South Carolina During Reconstruction, 1861-1877.* Chapel Hill: University of North Carolina Press, 1965.

Wilson, Charles Reagan, ed. *The New Encyclopedia of Southern Culture Myth, Manners, and Memory.* Chapel Hill: University of North Carolina Press, 2006.

Woodward, C. Vann. *Origins of the New South: 1877-1913.* Baton Rouge: Louisiana State University Press, 1951.

--------. *Reunion and Reaction: The Compromise of 1877 and the End of Reconstruction.* New York: Oxford University Press, 1991.

Young, Jeffrey Robert. *Domesticating Slavery: The Master Class in Georgia and South Carolina, 1670-1830. Chapel Hill: University of North Carolina Press, 1999.*

ARTICLES

Alston, Lee J. and Joseph P. Ferrie, "Paternalism in Agricultural Labor Contracts in the U.S. South: Implications for the Growth of the Welfare State." *The American Economic Review* 83 (September 1993): 852-876.

Bacot, D. Huger. "The South Carolina Up Country at the End of the Eighteenth Century." *The American Historical Review* 28 (July 1923): 682-698.

Bledsoe , Jerry. "Dooty's Last Stand." *Southern Changes*, (October-November 1978): 13-15.

Carlson, Douglas W. "Drinks to His Own Undoing': Temperance Ideology in the Deep South." Journal *of the Early Republic* 18 (Winter 1998): 659-91.

Carlton, David L. and Peter A. Coclanis, "Capital Mobilization and Southern Industry, 1880-1905: The Case of the Carolina Piedmont." *The Journal of Economic History* 49 (March 1989): 73-94.

Christensen, Niels Jr. "The State Dispensaries of South Carolina." *Annals of the American Academy of Political and Social Science* 32 (November 1908): 75-85.

Davis, Robert S. "The North Georgia Moonshine War of 1876-1877." *North Georgia Journal* 6 (Autumn 1989): 42-45.

Downey, Tom "Riparian Rights and Manufacturing in Antebellum South Carolina: William Gregg and the Origins of the 'Industrial Mind'." *The Journal of Southern History* 65 (February 1999), 77-108.

Edwards, John C. "Doughboys and Spartans: The Story of Camp Wadsworth." *South Carolina History Illustrated* 1 (Winter 1970): 4-8, 61-67.

Eelman, Bruce "Entrepreneurs in the Southern Upcountry: The Case of Spartanburg, South Carolina, 1815-1880." Enterprise and Society: *The International Journal of Business History* 5 (Spring 2004): 77-106.

Emory, S. T. "Topography and Towns of the Carolina Piedmont." *Economic Geography* 12 (January 1936): 91-97.

Ford, Lacy K. "Rednecks and Merchants: Economic Development and Social Tensions in the South Carolina Upcountry, 1865-1900." *The Journal of American History* 71 (September 1984): 294-318.

Gallay, Allan "The Origins of Slaveholders' Paternalism: George Whitefield, the Bryan Family, and the Great Awakening in the South." *The Journal of Southern History* 53 (August 1987): 369-394.

Grundy, Pamela. "We Always Tried to Be Good People": Respectability, Crazy Water Crystals, and Hillbilly Music on the Air, 1933-1935." *The Journal of American History* 81 (March 1995): 1591-1620.

Holmes, William F. "Moonshining and Collective Violence: Georgia, 1889-1895." *Journal of American History* 67 (December 1980): 589-611.

Kennett, Lee. "The Camp Wadsworth Affair." *Southern Atlantic Quarterly* 74 (Summer 1974); 197-211.

Kibler, Lillian A. "Unionist Sentiment in South Carolina in 1860." *The Journal of Southern History* 4 (August 1938): 346-366.

Klotter, James C. "The Black South and White Appalachia." *The Journal of American History* 66 (March 1980): 832-849.

Lander, Ernest M. Jr. "Manufacturing in South Carolina, 1815-60." *The Business History Review* 28 (March 1954): 59-66.

Langrall, Peggy. "Appalachian Folk Music: From Foothills to Footlights." *Music Educators Journal* 72 (March 1986): 37-39.

Marrs, Aaron. "Dissatisfaction and Desertion in Greenville District, South Carolina: 1860-1865." *The Proceedings of the South Carolina Historical Association* (2001): 39-50.

Miller, Wilbur R. "The Revenue: Federal Law Enforcement in the Mountain South, 1870-1900." *The Journal of Southern History* 55 (May, 1989): 195-216.

Parker, Lewis W. "Condition of Labor in Southern Cotton Mills." *Annals of the American Academy of Political and Social Science* 33 (March 1909): 54-62.

Peterson, Betty. "Why They Talk That Talk: Language in Appalachian Studies." *The English Journal* 76 (October 1987): 53-56.

Poole, W. Scott. "Religion, Gender, and the Lost Cause in South Carolina's 1876 Governor's Race: 'Hampton or Hell!'." *The Journal of Southern History* 68 (August 2002): 573-598

Schmidt, Charles W. "Sprawl: The New Manifest Destiny?" *Environmental Health Perspectives* 112 (August 2004): 620-627.

Schultz, Stanly K. "Temperance Reform in the Antebellum South: Social Control and Urban Order." *South Atlantic Quarterly* 83 (Summer 1984): 322-39.

Sharpless, Rebecca. "Southern Women and the Land," *Agricultural History* 67 (Spring 1993): 30-42.

Simon, Bryant "The Appeal of Cole Bleese of South Carolina: Race, Class, and Sex in the New South." *The Journal of Southern History* 62, (February 1996): 57-86.

Stewart, Bruce E. "Select Men of Sober and Industrious Habits: Alcohol Reform and Social Conflict in Antebellum Appalachia." *The Journal of Southern History* 73 (May 2007): 289-322.

Täng, Anthony M. "Farm Income Differentials in the Southern Piedmont, 1860-1940." *Southern Economic Journal* 23 (July 1956): 1-14.

Terrill, Tom E. Edmond Ewing and Pamela White, "Eager Hands: Labor for Southern Textiles, 1850-1860." *The Journal of Economic History* 36 (March 1976): 84-99.

Tyrell, Ian R. "Drink and Temperance in the Antebellum South: An Overview and Interpretation." *Journal of Southern History* 48 (November 1982): 485-510.

Williams, Jack Kenny. "White Lawbreakers in Ante-Bellum South Carolina." *The Journal of Southern History* 21 (August 1955): 360-373.

NEWSPAPERS

Anderson (SC) Intelligencer

Charleston (SC) City Gazette and Daily Advertiser

Charleston (SC) Courier

Charleston (SC) News and Courier

Charleston (SC) State Gazette of South Carolina

Charleston (SC) South Carolina Gazette

Columbia (SC) The State

Greenville (SC) Daily News

Greenville (SC) Enterprise

Greenville (SC) Enterprise and Mountaineer

Greenville (SC) Mountaineer

Greenville (SC) News

Greenville (SC) Piedmont

Greer (SC) Greer Citizen

New York (NY) Times

Pickens (SC) Sentinel

Spartanburg (SC) Carolina Spartan

Spartanburg (SC) Express

Spartanburg (SC) Journal

Spartanburg (SC) Piedmont Headlight

Tryon (NC) Daily Bulletin

UNPUBLISHED MATERIALS

Cresswell, Stephen "Resistance and Enforcement: The U.S. Department of Justice, 1870-1893." Ph.D. dissertation, University of Virginia, 1986.

Eelman, Bruce William. "Progress and Community From Old South to New South: Spartanburg County, South Carolina, 1845-1880." Ph.D. dissertation, University of Maryland, 2000.

Hamm, Richard. "Origins of the Eighteenth Amendment: Prohibition in the Federal System, 1880-1920." Ph.D. dissertation, University of Virginia, 1987

Mittleman, Amy H. "The Politics of Alcohol Production: The Liquor Industry and the Federal Government, 1862-1900." Ph.D. dissertation, Columbia University, 1986.

WEB RESOURCES

Cliffs at Glassy. "SC country club living." http://www.cliffscommunities.com/cliffs-living/ [accessed March 19, 2008].

Foothills Trail Conference. "A 76 mile woodland path along the Blue Ridge Escarpment in northwestern South Carolina." http://www.foothillstrail.org/ [accessed March 19, 2008].

Greenville Chamber of Commerce. "Quality of Life in Greenville." http://www.greenvillechamber.org [accessed March 27, 2008].

Hidden Hills of Glassy Mountain. "Discover the Hidden Glory."
http://www.hiddenhillsofglassymtn.com/ [accessed March 27,
2008].

Tryon Real Estate. "Rustic Mountain Living." http://www.tryon-
real-estate-and-homes.com/cliffs/ [accessed March 27, 2008].

End Notes

Notes to the Introduction

[1] *Greenville (SC) Enterprise and Mountaineer*, 26 August 1891.

[2] Ibid.

[3] Ibid.

[4] Ibid.

[5] Ibid.

[6] Mann Batson, *The Upper Part of Greenville County, South Carolina* (Taylors, SC: Faith Printing Company, 1993), 458-459.

[7] Lacy K. Ford. *Origins of Southern Radicalism: The South Carolina Upcountry, 1800-1860* (New York: Oxford University Press, 1988), 239-240.

[8] Archie Vernon Huff Jr., *Greenville: The History of the City and County in the South Carolina Piedmont* (Columbia: University of South Carolina Press, 1995), 218.

[9] For detailed analysis of Appalachian culture and perceptions of it see John Alexander Williams, *Appalachia: A History* (Chapel Hill: University of North Carolina Press, 2002); **Mary Beth Pudup, Dwight B. Billings, Altina L. Waller, eds.,** *Appalachia in the Making: the Mountain South in the Nineteenth Century* **(Chapel Hill: University of North Carolina Press, 1995); Henry D. Shapiro,** *Appalachia on Our Mind: the Southern Mountains and Mountaineers in American Consciousness, 1870-1920* **(Chapel Hill: University of North Carolina Press, 1978); Jack E. Weller,** *Yesterday's People: Life in Contemporary Appalachia* **(Lexington: University of Kentucky Press, 1965); John B. Rehder,** *Appalachian Folkways* **(Baltimore: John Hopkins University Press, 2004); W.K. McNeil,**

ed., *Appalachian Images in Folk and Popular Culture* **(Knoxville: University of Tennessee Press, 1995); Jane S. Becker,** *Selling Tradition : Appalachia and the Construction of an American folk, 1930-1940* **(Chapel Hill: University of North Carolina Press, 1998); Horace Kephart,** *Our Southern Highlanders: a Narrative of Adventure in the Southern Appalachians and a Study of Life Among the Mountaineers* **(Knoxville: University of Tennessee Press, 1984).**

[10] Richard B. Drake, *A History of Appalachia* (Lexington: University of Kentucky Press, 2001), 68-69.

[11] Drake, *History of Appalachia,* 68-69.

[12] James V. Gregory and James Walton Lawrence Sr., *Indians, Bloodshed, Tears, Churches, & Schools: It all Started at Fort Gowan* (Landrum, South Carolina: Lawrence, 2003), 31; D. Huger Bacot, "The South Carolina Up Country at the End of the Eighteenth Century," *The American Historical Review*, 28 (July 1923): 685.

[13] Drake, *History of Appalachia,* 85-86; William W. Freehling, *Prelude to Civil War: The Nullification Controversy in South Carolina, 1816-1836* (New York: Oxford University Press, 1965), 18; James V. Gregory and James Walton Lawrence Sr., *Indians, Bloodshed, Tears, Churches, & Schools: It all Started at Fort Gowan* (Landrum, South Carolina: Lawrence, 2003), 31; D. Huger Bacot, "The South Carolina Up Country at the End of the Eighteenth Century," *The American Historical Review*, 28 (July 1923): 685.

[14] Drake, *History of Appalachia,* 71-72; Rebecca Sharpless, "Southern Women and the Land," *Agricultural History,* 67 (Spring 1993): 38-41; for a detailed analysis of Lowcountry yeoman that bought into the dominate ideology of South Carolina see Stephanie McCurry, *Masters of Small Worlds: Yeoman Households, Gender Relations, and the Political Culture of the Antebellum South Carolina Low Country* (New York: Oxford University Press, 1997).

[15] *Greenville (SC) Enterprise and Mountaineer.* 8 October 1890.

[16] H. Tyler Blethen and Curtis W. Wood Jr., ed., *Ulster and North America: Transatlantic Perspectives on the Scotch*-Irish (Tuscaloosa: University of Alabama

Press, 2007), 213, 215, 217.

[17] Cratis D. Williams, *Southern Mountain Speech* (Berea, Kentucky: Berea College Press, 1992), 1, 17, 28.

[18] Michael Montgomery and Ellen Johnson, eds., *The New Encyclopedia of Southern Culture: Language* (Chapel Hill: University of North Carolina Press, 2007), 43; see also Michael Montgomery, *From Ulster to America: The Scotch-Irish Heritage of American English* (Belfast: Ulster Historical Foundation, 2004); Michael Montgomery, *The Dictionary of Smoky Mountain English* (Knoxville: University of Tennessee Press, 2004).

[19] Ibid.; Betty Peterson, "Why They Talk That Talk: Language in Appalachian Studies," *The English Journal* 76 (October 1987): 54.

[20] Jerry Bledsoe, "Dooty's Last Stand," *Southern Changes*, October-November 1978, 13.

[21] John C. Campbell, *The Southern Highlander and His Homeland* (Lexington: University of Kentucky Press, 1969), 91.

[22] Campbell, *Southern Highlander,* 116-119.

[23] Lawrence, *Smokin' Shootin' Irons,* 7; *Charleston (SC) City Gazette and Daily Advertiser* 29 November 1797.

[24] *Greenville (SC) Enterprise and Mountaineer,* 15 February 1888.

[25] For a description of violence in South Carolina culture see Jack Kenny Williams, "White Lawbreakers in Ante-Bellum South Carolina," *The Journal of Southern History* 21 (August 1955): 360-373.

[26] Charles Reagan Wilson, ed., *The New Encyclopedia of Southern Culture Myth, Manners, and Memory* (Chapel Hill: University of North Carolina Press, 2006), 226-227.

[27] Huff, *Greenville,* 218.

[28] For more on Southern cultural traits of violence see John Hope Franklin, *The Militant South* (Cambridge: Belknap Press of Harvard University, 1956); Edward Ayers, *Vengeance and Justice: Crime and Punishment in the 19th Century American South* (New York: Oxford University Press, 1984).

[29] Batson, *The Upper Part of* Greenville, 458-459.

[30] Huff, *Greenville*, 142.

[31] *Grenville (SC) Mountaineer*, 19 November 1898.

[32] New *York Times*, 4 March 1900.

[33] While local genealogist and amateur historians have attempted to outline the history of the Dark Corner, at present there have not been any attempt to study Appalachian culture, violence, and its relationship to illicit distillation in the Dark Corner. For more information see Walter Edgar, ed., *The South Carolina Encyclopedia (Columbia: University of South Carolina Press, 2006), 245; Batson, The Upper Part of Greenville County, 458-459;* Huff, *Greenville,* 142; J. Dean Crain, *A Mountain Boy's Life Story* (Greenville, SC: Baptist Courier, 1914); James Walton Lawrence Sr., *Hogback Country* (Landrum, SC: News Leader, 1982).

Notes to Chapter One

[34] Lawrence, *Smokin' Shootin' Irons*, 1.

[35] Batson, *The Upper Part of Greenville*, 457.

[36] *Greenville (SC) Enterprise and Mountaineer,* 29 November 1893.

[37] *(SC) Pickens Sentinel*, 18 January 1877.

[38] *Greenville (SC) Mountaineer*, 23 January 1897.

[39] Batson, *The Upper Part of Greenville,* 457.

[40] *New York Times*, 4 March 1900.

[41] *(SC) Greenville Daily News*, 29 May 1894.

[42] For more see Freehling, *Prelude to Civil War;* Lillian Adele Kibler, *Benjamin F. Perry: South Carolina Unionist* (Durham: Duke University Press, 1946).

[43] Quoted in Batson, *The Upper Part of Greenville*, 459.

[44] Ibid.

[45] James A. Howard, *Dark Corner Heritage* (Self Published, 1980), 2.

[46] Anne H. Hendricks, *The Dark Corner of Greenville* County. Edited By Jeffry R. Willis . Greenville: The Greenville County Historical Society, 1998., 87.

[47] *Greenville (SC) Mountaineer*, 13 July 1849.

[48] Drake, *History of Appalachia*, 35-36.

[49] James Walton Lawrence Sr., *The Shadows of Hogback* (Landrum, SC: The News Leader, 1979.), 4.

[50] Huff , *Greenville*, 18-19.

[51] Huff, *Greenville*, 14-16.

[52] *Charleston (SC) State Gazette of South Carolina*, 22 March 1792; *Charleston (SC) South Carolina Gazette*, 5 April 1792.

[53] *Greenville (SC) Mountaineer*, 13 July 1849.

[54] Lillian A. Kibler, "Unionist Sentiment in South Carolina in 1860," *The Journal of Southern History* 4 (August 1938): 355; *Spartanburg (SC) Express,* 17 October 1860; *Charleston (SC) Courier,* 24 October 1860.

[55] For further information on Greenville County desertions from Confederate service see Aaron Marrs, "Dissatisfaction and Desertion in Greenville District, South Carolina: 1860-1865," *The Proceedings of The South Carolina Historical Association*, (2001): 39-50.

[56] Huff, *Greenville*, 136.

[57] Ibid., 27-28.

[58] Lawrence, *Smokin' Shootin' Irons*, 74.

[59] For more information on Unionist sentiment and dissatisfaction with the Confederate government in the Blue Ridge see John C. Inscoe and Gordon B. McKinney, "Highland House Households Divided: Family Deceptions, Diversions and Divisions in Southern Appalachia's Inner Civil War," and Keith S. Bohannon, "They Had Determined to Root Us Out: Dual Memoirs by a Unionist Couple in Blue Ridge Georgia," in John C. Inscoe and Robert Kenzer, eds. *Enemies of the Country: New Perspectives on Unionist in the Civil War South* (Athens: University of Georgia Press, 2001); Richard Nelson Current, *Lincoln's Loyalist: Union Soldiers from the Confederacy* (Lebanon, New Hampshire: University Press of New England, 1992).

[60] Huff, *Greenville*, 142.

[61] Jerry Hughes. *Once Upon a Time in Pickens County: The Amos Ladd and Lewis R. Redmond Story* (Self Published, 1993), 34.

[62] *Greenville (SC) Enterprise and Mountaineer*, 15 February 1888.

[63] Drake, *History of Appalachia*, 109-111.

[64] *Greenville (SC) Mountaineer*, 29 November 1893; *(NC) Tryon Daily Bulletin*, 26 August 1974.

[65] Batson, *The Upper Part of Greenville*, 467-468.

[66] *Greenville (SC) Enterprise and Mountaineer*, 6 October 1875.

[67] *Greenville (SC) Greenville News*, 30 June 1935.

[68] William Scott Poole, *Never Surrender: Confederate Memory and Conservation in the South Carolina Upcountry* (Athens: University of Georgia Press, 2004), 21-22; For definition and depth of the Paternalist culture in South Carolina see Allan Gallay, "The Origins of Slaveholders' Paternalism: George Whitefield, the Bryan Family, and the Great Awakening in the South," *The Journal of Southern History* 53 (August 1987): 369-394; Jeffrey Robert Young, *Domesticating Slavery: The Master Class in Georgia and South Carolina, 1670-1837 (Chapel Hill: University of North Carolina Press, 1999);* Lee J. Alston and Joseph P. Ferrie, "Paternalism in Agricultural Labor Contracts in the U.S. South: Implications for the Growth of the Welfare State," *The American Economic Review* 83 (September 1993): 852-876; Lee J. Alston and Joseph P. Ferrie, *Southern Paternalism and the American Welfare State: Economics, Politics, and Institutions in the South, 1865-1965 (New York: Cambridge University Press, 1999); Stephen Kantrowitz, Ben Tillman & the Reconstruction of White Supremacy (Chapel Hill: University of North Carolina Press, 2000).*

[69] Drake, *History of Appalachia, 91.*

[70] Batson, *The Upper Part of Greenville*, 458-459.

[71] Howard, *Dark Corner Heritage*, 2; Huff, *Upper Part of Greenville*, 132, 136.

[72] Ford, *Origins of Southern Radicalism*, 57.

[73] Ibid., 47; Wilbur R. Miller, *Revenuers & Moonshiners: Enforcing Federal Liquor Law in the Mountain South, 1865-1900* (Chapel Hill: The University of North

Carolina Press, 1991), 19; William W. Freehling, *The South vs. The South :How Anti-confederate Southerners Shaped the Course of the Civil War* (New York: Oxford University Press, 2001), 22-23.

[74] Ford, *Origins of Southern Radicalism,* 216, 221, 225, 228; S. T. Emory, "Topography and Towns of the Carolina Piedmont," *Economic Geography* 12 (January 1936): 91-93.

[75] Ford, *Origins of Southern Radicalism,* 57.

[76] Huff, *Greenville,* 218.

[77] *Greenville (SC) Enterprise and Mountaineer,* 1 July 1891; Anthony M. Täng, "Farm Income Differentials in the Southern Piedmont, 1860-1940," *Southern Economic Journal* 23 (July 1956): 4, 6-7.

[78] *New York Times,* 4 March 1900.

[79] David W. Maurer, *Kentucky Moonshine* (Lexington: University of Kentucky Press, 1974), 12-16.

[80] Wilbur R. Miller, *Revenuers and Moonshiners: Enforcing Federal Liquor Law in the Mountain South, 1865-1900.* (Chapel Hill: The University of North Carolina Press, 1991), 28; *Greenville (SC) Enterprise and Mountaineer* 27 November 1889.

[81] Maurer, 25.

[82] *New York Times.* 27 January 1888.

[83] David W. Maurer, *Kentucky Moonshine* (Lexington: University of Kentucky Press, 1974), 12-16; William Hogeland, *The Whiskey Rebellion: George Washington, Alexander Hamilton, and the Frontier Rebels who Challenged America's Newfound Sovereignty* (New York: Scribner, 2006), 66-67.

[84] *Greenville (SC) Mountaineer,* 13 July 1849; Anne McCuen. 1983. Interviewed by Dean Campbell. Greenville, SC. June 2, transcript, Tales From the Dark Corner: Documenting the Oral Tradition (Hereafter referred to as TDC), Greenville County Library, SC.

[85] For detailed descriptions of the home distillation process and its history see Jess Carr, *The Second Oldest Profession: An Informal History of Moonshining in America* (Englewood Cliffs, New Jersey: Prentice-Hall, 1972); Joseph Earl Dabney,

Mountain Sprits: A Chronicle of Corn Whiskey From King James' Ulster Plantation to America's Appalachians and the Moonshine Life (Asheville, North Carolina: Bright Mountain Books, 1974); Joseph Earl Dabney, *More Mountain Sprits: The Continuing Chronicle of Moonshine Life and Corn Whiskey, Wines, Ciders &Beers in America's Appalachians* (Asheville, North Carolina: Bright Mountain Books, 1980); Esther Kellner, *Moonshine: Its History and Folklore* (New York: Weathervane Books, 1971); Gerald Carson , *The Social History of Bourbon: An Unhurried Account of Our Star-Spangled American* Drink (New York: Dodd, Mead, 1963); David W. Maurer, *Kentucky Moonshine.*

[86] *Greenville (SC) Greenville Daily News*, 29 May 1894.

[87] *New York Times*, 4 March 1900.

Notes to Chapter Two

[88] *Spartanburg (SC) Carolina Spartan*, 3 January 1867.

[89] Miller, *Revenuers & Moonshiners,* 61; Bruce William Eelman, "Progress and Community From Old South to New South: Spartanburg County, South Carolina, 1845-1880" (PhD. diss., University of Maryland, 2000), 366-67, 383-4, 393-94.

[90] Dabney, *Mountain Spirits,* 74.

[91] For information on the postwar Internal Revenue Service see Richard Hamm, " Origins of the Eighteenth Amendment: Prohibition in the Federal System, 1880-1920, " Ph.D. dissertation, University of Virginia, 1987; Frederic C. Howe, *Taxation and Taxes in the United States Under the Internal Revenue System, 1791-1895* (New York: T. Y. Crowell, 1896); Tun Yuan Hu, *The Liquor Tax in the United States, 1791-1947: A History of the Internal Revenue Taxes Imposed on Distilled Spirits by the Federal Government* (New York: Graduate School of Business, Columbia University, 1950); Amy H. Mittleman, "The Politics of Alcohol Production: The Liquor Industry and the Federal Government, 1862-1900," Ph.D. dissertation, Columbia University, 1986; Laurence F. Schmeckebier and Francis X. Eble, *The Bureau of Internal Revenue: Its History, Activities and Organization* (Baltimore:

John Hopkins University Press, 1923); Miller, *Revenuers and Moonshiners,* 5-6; Miller makes note on page 190 of his work that very little attention has been paid by professional historians towards revenue enforcement and their fight with the moonshiners during the Reconstruction era or afterwards.

[92] Miller, *Revenuers & Moonshiners,* 62.

[93] Dabney, *Mountain Spirits,* 74.

[94] Drake, *History of Appalachia,* 109.

[95] Batson, *The Upper Part of Greenville,* 496-497.

[96] Poole, *Never Surrender,* 105-107. For more information on the Reconstruction era see E. Merton Coulter, *The South During Reconstruction, 1865-1877* (Baton Rouge: Louisiana State University Press, 1947); Eric Foner, *America's Reconstruction: People and Politics After the Civil War* (Baton Rouge: Louisiana State University Press, 1997); Joel Williamson, *After Slavery: the Negro in South Carolina During Reconstruction, 1861-1877* (Chapel Hill: University of North Carolina Press, 1965).

[97] Miller, *Revenuers & Moonshiners,* 49; For information on the organization, depth, and goals of the Redeemer movement see Poole, *Never Surrender;* W. Scott Poole, "Religion, Gender, and the Lost Cause in South Carolina's 1876 Governor's Race: 'Hampton or Hell!'," *The Journal of Southern History* 68 (August 2002): 573-598; Edmund L. Drago, *Hurrah For Hampton: Black Red Shirts in South Carolina During Reconstruction* (Fayetteville: University of Arkansas Press, 1998); Walter Edgar, *South Carolina: A History* (Columbia: University of South Carolina Press, 1998.), 377-406

[98] Hughes, *Once Upon a Time in Pickens County,* 36.

[99] Poole, *Never Surrender,* 107.

[100] Lucius C. Northrop, to Governor Wade Hampton, May 6, 1878. F 602745 Letters Received by the Department of South Carolina, 1871-1884 micro. National Archives and Records Administration (hereafter referred to as NARA), Washington D. C.

[101] For information on the Revenue War throughout the rest of Southern Appalachia see Miller, *Revenuers & Moonshiners;* Wilbur R. Miller, "The Revenue:

Federal Law Enforcement in the Mountain South, 1870-1900," *The Journal of Southern History* 55 (May, 1989): 195-216.

[102] *New York Times*, 27 January 1888.

[103] Miller, *Revenuers & Moonshiners*, 70-72.

[104] Ibid., 81, 100.

[105] For more on postwar resistance to Federal law enforcement see Stephen Cresswell, "Resistance and Enforcement: The U.S. Department of Justice, 1870-1893," (Ph.D. dissertation, University of Virginia, 1986).

[106] Miller, *Revenuers & Moonshiners*, 129.

[107] Ibid., 103; Poole, *Never Surrender*, 106.

[108] Davis v. South Carolina, 107 U. S. 597 (1883)

[109] *Greenville (SC) Enterprise*, 5 June 1872; Miller, *Revenuers & Moonshiners*, 42.

[110] Miller, *Revenuers & Moonshiners*, 42, 100-101.

[111] Robert S. Davis, "The North Georgia Moonshine War of 1876-1877," *North Georgia Journal* 6 (Autumn 1989): 42-45; For more on moonshiner resistance in North Georgia see William F. Holmes, "Moonshining and Collective Violence: Georgia, 1889-1895," *Journal of American History* 67 (December 1980): 589-611.

[112] Miller, *Revenuers & Moonshiners*, 127-128.

[113] Miller, *Revenuers & Moonshiners*, 129.

[114] Miller, *Revenuers & Moonshiners*, 110-111.

[115] Hughes, *Once Upon a Time in Pickens County*, 63.

[116] *Greenville (SC) Enterprise and Mountaineer*, 16 March 1887.

[117] Miller, *Revenuers & Moonshiners*, 108-109.

[118] Lawrence, *Smokin' Shootin' Irons*, 16.

[119] *Greenville (SC) Enterprise and Mountaineer*, 18 March 1877.

[120] For more on white solidarity and supremacy see Kantrowitz, *Ben Tillman & the Reconstruction of White Supremacy*.

[121] Robert M. Wallace, to Hon. Charles Devens, September 13, 1877, F 602745 Letters Received by the Department of South Carolina, 1871-1884 micro. NARA.

[122] Miller, *Revenuers & Moonshiners*, 80.

[123] *Greenville (SC) Enterprise and Mountaineer,* 21 February 1877.

[124] Robert M. Wallace, to Hon. Charles Devens, December 31, 1877. F 602745 Letters Received by the Department of South Carolina, 1871-1884 micro. NARA.

[125] Ibid.

[126] Robert M. Wallace, to Hon. Charles Devens, December 15,1877. F 602745 Letters Received by the Department of South Carolina, 1871-1884 micro. NARA.

[127] Miller, *Revenuers & Moonshiners,* 47-50.

[128] Hughes, *Once Upon a Time in Pickens County,* 6.

[129] For more on the Lewis Redmond's exploits see Jerry Hughes, *Once Upon A Time in Pickens County: the Amos Ladd and Lewis Redmond Story* (Self Published, 1993).

[130] Robert M. Wallace, to Hon. Charles Devens, December 15,1877. F 602745 Letters Received by the Department of South Carolina, 1871-1884 micro. NARA.

[131] Ibid.

[132] Ibid.

[133] Lucius C. Northrop, to Hon. Charles Devens, April 22, 1878. F 602745 Letters Received by the Department of South Carolina, 1871-1884 micro. NARA.; *Greenville (SC) Enterprise and Mountaineer,* 16 March 1887.

[134] G.P. Kirkland, to Lucius C. Northrop, January 20, 1878. F 602745 Letters Received by the Department of South Carolina, 1871-1884 micro. NARA.; *Greenville (SC) Enterprise and Mountaineer,* 15 February 1888.

[135] Lucius C. Northrop, to Hon. Charles Devens, April 25, 1878. F 602745 Letters Received by the Department of South Carolina, 1871-1884 micro. NARA.

[136] Lucius C. Northrop, to Governor Wade Hampton, May 6, 1878. F 602745 Letters Received by the Department of South Carolina, 1871-1884 micro. NARA.

[137] Hughes, *Once Upon a Time in Pickens County,* 30.

[138] Poole, *Never Surrender,* 108.

[139] *Pickens (SC) Pickens Sentinel,* 13 June 1878, *Greenville (SC) Enterprise and Mountaineer,* 12 June 1878, *Greenville (SC) Enterprise and Mountaineer,* 10 July 1878, *Greenville (SC) Enterprise and Mountaineer,* 17 July 1878, *Greenville (SC) Enterprise and Mountaineer,* 31 July 1878.

[140] Ibid.

[141] Ibid.

[142] Hughes, *Once Upon a Time in Pickens* County, 47-49.

[143] Hughes, *Once Upon a Time in Pickens County,* 49.

[144] Lucius C. Northrop, to Hon. Charles Devens, June 12, 1878. F 602745 Letters Received by the Department of South Carolina, 1871-1884 micro. NARA.

[145] Hughes, *Once Upon a Time in Pickens County,* 47-48.

[146] Lucius C. Northrop, to Hon. Charles Devens, June 12, 1878. F 602745 Letters Received by the Department of South Carolina, 1871-1884 micro. NARA.

[147] Ibid.

[148] *Greenville (SC) Enterprise and Mountaineer,* 17 July 1878.

[149] *Pickens (SC) Pickens Sentinel,* 15 August 1878.

[150] *Greenville (SC) Enterprise and Mountaineer,* 31 July 1878. For more on Hayes and his election see C. Vann Woodward, *Reunion and Reaction: The Compromise of 1877and the End of Reconstruction* (New York: Oxford University Press, 1991)

[151] Miller, *Revenuers & Moonshiners,* 135.

[152] Greenville, SC, to Hon. Charles Devens, August 6, 1878. F 602745 Letters Received by the Department of South Carolina, 1871-1884 micro. NARA.

[153] Marshal R. M. Wallace, to Hon. Charles Devens, August 7, 1878. F 602745 Letters Received by the Department of South Carolina, 1871-1884 micro. NARA.

[154] Ibid.

[155] Miller, *Revenuers & Moonshiners,* 135.

[156] Ibid.

[157] Lucius C. Northrop, to Hon. Charles Devens, August 7, 1878. F 602745 Letters Received by the Department of South Carolina, 1871-1884 micro. NARA.

[158] Miller, *Revenuers & Moonshiners,* 116-117.

[159] Lucius C. Northrop, to Hon. Charles Devens, July 25, 1879. F 602745 Letters Received by the Department of South Carolina, 1871-1884 micro. NARA.

Notes to Chapter Three

[160] Ms. Saunders' inspiration for this illustration is due in part to a drawing by Lyndall Mason featured in Jess Carr's, *The Second Oldest Profession: An Informal History of Moonshining in America* (Englewood Cliffs, New Jersey: Prentice-Hall, 1972), 75.

[161] *Greenville (SC) Enterprise,* 1 February 1871; 10 February 1875; 4 August 1875; 13 February 1878; 28 August 1878; 30 March 1881; James C. Klotter, "The Black South and White Appalachia," *The Journal of American History* 66 (March 1980): 833.

[162] David L. Carlton and Peter A. Coclanis, "Capital Mobilization and Southern Industry, 1880-1905: The Case of the Carolina Piedmont," *The Journal of Economic History* 49 (March 1989): 73-74.

[163] Howard N. Rabinowitz, *The First New South, 1865-1920* (Arlington Heights, Illinois: Harlan Davidson, 1992), 50-51, 53.

[164] C. Van Woodward, *Origins of the New South: 1877- 1913* (Baton Rouge: Louisiana State University Press, 1951), 60; For more on South Carolina politics and developments during later decades of the nineteenth century see William J. Cooper, *The Conservative Regime: South Carolina, 1877-1890* (Baltimore: John Hopkins University Press, 1968).

[165] Woodward, *Origins of the New South,* 131-132, 140; Lacy K. Ford, "Rednecks and Merchants: Economic Development and Social Tensions in the South Carolina Upcountry, 1865-1900," *The Journal of American History* 71 (September 1984): 298-299.

[166] For a comprehensive account of the development and industrialization of Greenville County's eastern neighbor see Bruce William Eelman, "Progress and Community From Old South to New South: Spartanburg County, South Carolina, 1845-1880" (PhD. diss., University of Maryland, 2000); Bruce Eelman, "Entrepreneurs in the Southern Upcountry: The Case of Spartanburg, South Carolina, 1815-1880," Enterprise and Society: *The International Journal of Business*

History 5 (Spring 2004): 77-106.

[167] Ray Belcher, *Greenville County, South Carolina: From Cotton Fields to Textile Center of the World* (Charleston, SC: History Press, 2006), 63.

[168] Belcher, *Greenville County, South Carolina,* 32; For information on antebellum cotton mills in South Carolina see Tom E. Terrill, Edmond Ewing and Pamela White, "Eager Hands: Labor for Southern Textiles, 1850-1860," *The Journal of Economic History* 36 (March 1976): 84-99; Tom Downey, "Riparian Rights and Manufacturing in Antebellum South Carolina: William Gregg and the Origins of the 'Industrial Mind'," *The Journal of Southern History* 65 (February 1999): 77-108.

[169] Woodward, *Origins of the New South*, 306-07; Rabinowitz, *The First New South,* 47; For a contemporary account of labor conditions in South Carolina according to industrialist and New South boosters see Lewis W. Parker, "Condition of Labor in Southern Cotton Mills," *Annals of the American Academy of Political and Social Science* 33 (March 1909): 54-62.

[170] Woodward, *Origins of the New South,* 306-307.

[171] Ibid., 417; Rabinowitz, *The First New South,* 43.

[172] David L Carlton, *Mill and Town in South Carolina: 1880-1920* (Baton Rouge: Louisiana State University Press, 1982.), 118-119.

[173] John J. Rumbarger, *Power, Profits, and Prohibition: Alcohol Reform and the Industrialization of America, 1800-1930* (Albany: State University of New York Press, 1989), xxi.

[174] Carlton, *Mill and Town,* 183; Cathy L. McHugh, "Schooling in the Post-Bellum Southern Cotton Mill Villages," *Journal of Social History* 20 (Autumn, 1986):149-161; For a revised view of mill labor paternalism and its limits see Mary Lether Wingerd, "Rethinking Paternalism: Power and Parochialism in a Southern Mill Village," *The Journal of American History* 83 (December 1996): 872-902; Poole, *Never Surrender,* 161-162.

[175] For more on the development of anti-drink reform in the South see Joe L. Coker, *Liquor in the Land of the Lost Cause: Southern White Evangelicals and the Prohibition Movement (Lexington: University of Kentucky Press, 2007).*

[176] Paul M. Gaston, *The New South Creed: A Study in Southern Mythmaking* (Baton Rouge: Louisiana State University Press, 1976), 204-05.

[177] For more on the transformation and development of Piedmont culture during the New South see Allen Tullos, *Habits of Industry: White Culture and the Transformation of the Carolina Piedmont* (Chapel Hill: University of North Carolina Press, 1989).

[178] Carlton, *Mill and Town,* 34.

[179] Ibid.

[180] *Greenville (SC) Enterprise and Mountaineer*, 11 September 1878.

[181] Carlton, *Mill and Town,* 83, 89-90.

[182] Edgar, *South Carolina*, 488; Carlton, *Mill and Town,* 9.

[183] Carlton, *Mill and Town,* 70-71.

[184] *Greenville (SC) Enterprise and Mountaineer*, 6 April 1881; W. J. Rorabaugh, *The Alcoholic Republic: An American Tradition* (New York: Oxford University Press, 1979), 188, 204.

[185] *Greenville (SC) Enterprise and Mountaineer*, 7 April 1880; For a more detailed description of Southern Temperance, its relationship to the middleclass, and its influence on industrialization see Bruce E. Stewart, "Select Men of Sober and Industrious Habits: Alcohol Reform and Social Conflict in Antebellum Appalachia," *The Journal of Southern History* 73 (May 2007): 289-322; Douglas W. Carlson, "Drinks to His Own Undoing': Temperance Ideology in the Deep South ," *Journal of the Early Republic* 18 (Winter 1998): 659-91; Stanly K. Schultz, "Temperance Reform in the Antebellum South: Social Control and Urban Order," *South Atlantic Quarterly* 83 (Summer 1984): 322-39; Ian R. Tyrell, "Drink and Temperance in the Antebellum South: An Overview and Interpretation," *Journal of Southern History* 48 (November 1982): 485-510.

[186] *Greenville (SC) Enterprise and Mountaineer*, 28 April 1875; 4 August 1875; 28 February 1877; 11 September 1878; 30 March 1881; 6 April 1881; 12 December 1883; 9 February 1887.

[187] *Greenville (SC) Mountaineer*, 19 January 1870; 20 April 1870; *Greenville (SC)*

Enterprise and Mountaineer, 10 March 1887; 18 April 1897; 15 February 1888; 26 August 1891; *Greenville (SC) Mountaineer,* 15 February 1893; 10 April 1893; 9 August 1893; 8 November 1893; 20 November 1893; 21 February 1894; 13 June 1894; 28 November 1894; 13 April 1895; 3 July 1895; 14 August 1897; 4 December 1897; 18 March 1900; 14 November 1900; 1 March 1902; 5 November 1902; 20 February 1904; 27 February 1904; *(SC) Greenville* News, 27 February 1906; *(SC) Greenville Daily* News, 13 July 1906; 14 February 1908; 19 June 1915.

[188] Carlton, *Mill and Town,* 148-149.

[189] *(SC) Pickens Sentinel,* 12 July 1877; Bruce E. Stewart, "Select Men of Sober and Industrious Habits: Alcohol Reform and Social Conflict in Antebellum Appalachia," *The Journal of Southern History* 73 (May 2007): 290-291.

[190] Stewart, "Select Men," 293.

[191] *Greenville (SC) Enterprise and Mountaineer,* 21 September 1870.

[192] *Greenville (SC) Enterprise,* 1 February 1871; *Greenville (SC) Enterprise and Mountaineer,* 10 February 1875; 4 August 1875; 13 February 1878; 28 August 1878; 30 March 1881; 12 December 1883; 9 February 1887; 16 February 1887; 9 March 1887; 16 March 1887; 3 August 1887; 10 August 1887.

[193] *Greenville (SC) Mountaineer,* 19 January 1870.

[194] *Greenville (SC) Enterprise,* 31 August 1870; *Greenville (SC) Enterprise & Mountaineer,* 28 February 1887; 10 August 1887; 17 August 1887; 15 February 1888; 15 February 1889; 20 February 1889; 28 August 1889; 5 February 1890; 18 November 1891; 7 February 1894; 15 August 1894.

[195] Huff, *Greenville,* 230-231.

[196] *Greenville (SC) Enterprise,* 21 September 1870.

[197] Huff, *Greenville,* 230-231.

[198] Ibid.

[199] Kantrowitz, *Ben Tillman & the Reconstruction of White Supremacy,* 183.

[200] Ibid., 190-191.

[201] For a contemporary study of the failures of the State Dispensary System see Niels Christensen, Jr., " The State Dispensaries of South Carolina," *Annals of the American*

Academy of Political and Social Science 32 (November 1908): 75-85.

[202] *Greenville (SC) Mountaineer*, 10 October 1894; 29 June 1895.

[203] *Greenville (SC) Mountaineer*, 8 November 1893.

[204] Kantrowitz, *Ben Tillman & the Reconstruction of White Supremacy*, 193-195.

[205] Kantrowitz, *Ben Tillman & the Reconstruction of White Supremacy*, 265.

[206] Carlton, *Mill and Town*, 258; Bryant Simon, "The Appeal of Cole Bleese of South Carolina: Race, Class, and Sex in the New South," *The Journal of Southern History* 62 (February 1996): 57-86.

[207] Phillip Kenneth Huggins, *The South Carolina Dispensary: a Bottle Collector's Atlas and History of the System* (Columbia: Sandlapper Press, 1971), 194; For more on progressive reforms during Manning's administration see Robert Milton Burts, *Richard Irvine Manning and the Progressive Movement in South Carolina* (Columbia: University of South Carolina Press, 1974).

[208] *Greenville (SC) Enterprise and Mountaineer*, 2 October 1889; Klotter, "Black South and White Appalachia," 839.

[209] Ibid.

[210] *Greenville (SC) Enterprise and Mountaineer*, 20 May 1891; Klotter, "Black South and White Appalachia," 846; Gaston, *The New South Creed*, 102-104.

[211] *Greenville (SC) Mountaineer*, 19 January 1870; 20 April 1870; *Greenville (SC) Enterprise and Mountaineer*, 10 March 1887; 18 April 1897; 15 February 1888; 26 August 1891; 15 February 1893; *Greenville (SC) Mountaineer*, 10 April 1893; 9 August 1893; 8 November 1893; 20 November 1893 21 February 1894; 13 June 1894 28 November 1894; 13 April 1895; 3 July 1895; 14 August 1897; 4 December 1897; 18 March 1900; 14 November 1900; 1 March 1902; 5 November 1902; 20 February 1904; 27 February 1904; *(SC) Greenville* News, 27 February 1906; 13 July 1906; 14 February 1908; 19 June 1915.

[212] Ibid.

[213] *Greenville (SC) Mountaineer*, 19 January 1870.

[214] *Greenville (SC) Enterprise*, 31 August 1870.

[215] Carlton, *Mill and Town*, 148-149.

[216] *Greenville (SC) Enterprise & Mountaineer*, 15 February 1888.

[217] Ibid.

[218] Ibid.

[219] Ibid.

[220] *(SC) Greenville Daily News*, 29 May 1894.

[221] *Greenville (SC) Mountaineer*, 19 November 1898.

[222] Miller, *Revenuers & Moonshiners*, 106.

[223] Carlton, *Mill and Town*, 148-149.

[224] *(SC) Greenville Daily News*, 3 July 1906.

[225] *Greenville (SC) Mountaineer*, 20 February 1904.

[226] *(SC) Greenville News*, 27 May 1906.

[227] Ibid.

[228] *Greenville (SC) Mountaineer*, 8 November 1893; *(SC) Greenville News*, 20 August 1905.

[229] Lawrence, *Smokin' Shootin' Irons* 115-120.

[230] For more on Camp Wadsworth and Camp Sevier in Greenville County see Archie Vernon Huff, *Greenville*, 284-285; Lee Kennett, "The Camp Wadsworth Affair," *Southern Atlantic Quarterly* 74 (Summer 1974): 197-211; John C. Edwards, "Doughboys and Spartans: The Story of Camp Wadsworth," *South Carolina History Illustrated* 1 (Winter 1970): 4-8, 61-67.

[231] Howard, *Dark Corner Heritage*, 47.

[232] George B. Tindall, *The Emergence of the New South, 1913-1945* (Baton Rouge: Louisiana State University Press, 1967), 53, 55-58.

[233] Alex Campbell. 1983. Interviewed by Dean Campbell, Glassy Mountain Township, SC, May 21, transcript, TDC.

[234] For more on national prohibition see Andrew Sinclair, *Prohibition: The Era of Excess* (Boston: Little & Brown, 1962); Edward Behr, *Prohibition: Thirteen Years that Changed America* (New York: Arcade Publishing, 1996); Kenneth M. Murchison, *Federal Criminal Law Doctrines: the Forgotten Influence of National Prohibition* (Durham, North Carolina: Duke University Press, 1994).

[235] *(SC) Greenville Piedmont*, 31 January 1929.

[236] For more on the end of Prohibition see David E. Kyvig, *Repealing Prohibition* (Kent, Ohio: Kent State University Press, 2000).

[237] *(NC) Tryon Daily Bulletin*, 26 August 1974.

[238] *(SC) Greenville News*, 3 May 1959.

[239] Thomas R. Allison. *Moonshine Memories* (Montgomery, Alabama: New South Books, 2001), 248-252; William L. Downard. *Dictionary of the History of the American Brewing and Distilling Industries* (Westport Connecticut: Greenwood Press, 1980), 238; Betty Boles Ellison. *Illegal Odyssey: 200 Years of Kentucky Moonshine* (Self-Published: Betty Boles Ellison, 2003), 135; *(SC) Spartanburg Journal* 21 November 1974.

[240] *(SC) Greenville News*, 10 May 1983; *(SC) Greenville Piedmont*, 18 April 1989.

Notes to Chapter Four

[241] *(SC) Greer Citizen*, 27 June 1990; *(SC) Greenville News*, 10 May 1983; Carlton, *Mill and Town*, 148-49; *(SC) Greenville* News, 2 February 1959; Pamela Grundy, "We Always Tried to Be Good People": Respectability, Crazy Water Crystals, and Hillbilly Music on the Air, 1933-1935," *The Journal of American History* 81 (March 1995): 1594, 1600-1601.

[242] *(SC) Spartanburg Journal*, 21 November 1974.

[243]Fay L. Lanford Sr. 1983. Interviewed by Bernard Zaidman. Gowansville, SC. July 14, transcript, TDC.

[244] *(SC) Greenville News*, 26 October 1970.

[245] Lester Brown. 1983. Interviewed by Bernard Zaidman. Glassy Mountain Township, SC. June 23, transcript, TDC.

[246] *(SC) Greenville News*, 30 June 1935; 2 February 1959; 29 January 1974; 10 May 1983; *(SC) Greenville Piedmont*, 18 April 1989.

[247] Bennie Lee Sinclair. 1986. Interviewed by Bernard Zaidman. Glassy Township, SC, June 9, transcript, TDC.

[248] Sinclair, interview, TDC.

[249] Drake, *History of Appalachia,* 225-226.

[250] Myrtle Lindsey. 1983. Interviewed by Bernard Zaidman. Glassy Township, SC, July 16, transcript, TDC.

[251] Lanford, interview, TDC.

[252] Arnold and Albert Emery. 1983. Interviewed by Bernard Zaidman. Glassy Mountain Township, SC. July 16, transcript, TDC.

[253] *(SC) Greenville News,* 10 May 1983.

[254] Junior and Sylvia Pitman. 1983. Interviewed by Bernard Zaidman. Glassy Mountain Township, SC, transcript, TDC.

[255] Ella Plumley. 1983. Interviewed by Bernard Zaidman. Glassy Mountain, Township, SC, June 23, transcript, TDC.

[256] Batson, *The Upper Part of Greenville,* 472-73.

[257] *(SC) Greenville Daily News,* 14 February 1908.

[258] For more on the view of informants in rural cultures see Robert James Scally, *The End of Hidden Ireland: Rebellion, Famine, & Emigration* (New York: Oxford University Press, 1995), 32, 37, 94, 97.

[259] Alex Campbell. 1983. Interviewed by Dean Campbell, Glassy Mountain Township, SC, May 21, transcript, TDC.

[260] Campbell, interview, TDC.

[261] For more on "pre-modern" ties to the land present in Appalachia through the twentieth century see Jack Temple Kirby, *Rural Lost Worlds: The American South, 1920-1960* (Baton Rouge: Louisiana State University Press, 1987), 118-122.

[262] Maynard and Randy Emery. 1983. Interviewed by Dean Campbell and Bernard Zaidman. Glassy Mountain Township, SC, June 25, transcript, TDC.

[263] James L. Hughes. 1983. Interviewed by Dean Campbell, Glassy Mountain Township, SC, May 21, transcript, TDC.

[264] *Greenville (SC) Mountaineer,* 19 April 1893.

[265] *Greenville (SC) Mountaineer,* 19 January 1870; 20 April 1870; *Greenville (SC) Enterprise and Mountaineer,* 10 March 1887; 18 April 1897; 15 February 1888;

26 August 1891; *Greenville (SC) Mountaineer,* 15 February 1893; 10 April 1893; 9 August 1893; 8 November 1893; 20 November 1893; 21 February 1894; 13 June 1894; 28 November 1894; 13 April 1895; 3 July 1895; 14 August 1897; 4 December 1897; 18 March 1900; 14 November 1900; 1 March 1902; 5 November 1902; 20 February 1904; 27 February 1904; *(SC) Greenville* News, 27 February 1906; 13 July 1906; 14 February 1908; 19 June 1915; 30 June 1935; 2 February 1959; 29 January 1974; 10 May 1983; *(SC) Greenville Piedmont,* 18 April 1989.

[266] Lester Brown. 1983. Interviewed by Bernard Zaidman. Glassy Mountain Township, SC. June 23, transcript, TDC; Fay L. Lanford Sr. 1983. Interviewed by Bernard Zaidman. Gowansville, SC. July 14, transcript, TDC; Campbell and Sons 1983. Interviewed by Bernard Zaidman. Glassy Mountain Township, SC. June 23, transcript, TDC; Alex Campbell. 1983. Interviewed by Bernard Zaidman. Glassy Mountain Township, SC. June 23, transcript, TDC; Pink and Ola Campbell. 1983. Interviewed by Bernard Zaidman. Glassy Mountain Township, SC. June 23, transcript, TDC; Albert Emery. 1983. Interviewed by Bernard Zaidman. Glassy Mountain Township, SC. June 23, transcript, TDC; Maynard Emory. 1983. Interviewed by Bernard Zaidman. Glassy Mountain Township, SC. June 23, transcript, TDC; Lois Harrison, James W. Harrison, T.A. Hyder. 1983. Interviewed by Bernard Zaidman. Glassy Mountain Township, SC. June 23, transcript, TDC; Alvin Howard. 1983. Interviewed by Bernard Zaidman. Glassy Mountain Township, SC. June 23, transcript, TDC; Dr. James Howard. 1983. Interviewed by Bernard Zaidman. Glassy Mountain Township, SC. June 23, transcript, TDC; James Hughes. 1983. Interviewed by Bernard Zaidman. Glassy Mountain Township, SC. June 23, transcript, TDC; Fay Lanford. 1983. Interviewed by Bernard Zaidman. Glassy Mountain Township, SC. June 23, transcript, TDC; Junior and Sylvia Pittman. 1983. Interviewed by Bernard Zaidman. Glassy Mountain Township, SC. June 23, transcript, TDC; Ella Plumley. 1983. Interviewed by Bernard Zaidman. Glassy Mountain Township, SC. June 23, transcript, TDC.

[267] *(SC) Greenville News,* 10 May 1983

[268] Campbell, interview, TDC.

[269] Ibid.

[270] Lester Brown, interview, TDC; Fay L. Lanford Sr., interview, TDC; Campbell and Sons ,interview, TDC; Alex Campbell, interview, TDC; Pink and Ola Campbell, interview, TDC; Albert Emory, interview, TDC; Maynard Emory, interview, TDC; Lois Harrison, James W. Harrison, T.A. Hyder, interview, TDC; Alvin Howard, interview, TDC; Dr. James Howard, interview, TDC; James Hughes, interview, TDC; Fay Lanford, interview, TDC; Junior and Sylvia Pittman, interview, TDC; Ella Plumley, interview, TDC.

[271] Lanford, interview, TDC.

[272] Miller. *Revenuers & Moonshiners*, 15.

[273] Emery, interview, TDC.

[274] *Greenville (SC) Enterprise and Mountaineer*, 18 March 1877.

[275] Emery, interview, TDC.

[276] Ibid.

[277] For more information on Appalachian ballads and rural southern music see Tristram Coffin, *The British Traditional Ballad in North America* (Philadelphia: American Folklore Society, 1963); Bill C. Malone, *Singing Cowboys and Musical Mountaineers: Southern Culture and the Roots of Country Music* (Athens: University of Georgia Press, 2003), 6-12; Peggy Langrall, "Appalachian Folk Music: From Foothills to Footlights," *Music Educators Journal* 72 (March 1986): 37-39.

[278] Emery, interview, TDC.

[279] Campbell, interview, TDC.

[280] *Greenville (SC) Mountaineer*, 19 November 1898; Campbell, interview, TDC.

[281] Emery, interview, TDC.

[282] Alvin Howard, interview, TDC.

[283] Lester Brown, interview, TDC.

[284] Durwood Dunn. *Cades Cove: The Life and Death of a Southern Appalachian Community, 1818-1937* (Knoxville: University of Tennessee Press, 1988), 233.

[285] *(SC) Greenville Daily News*, 20 February 1959.

[286] Emery, interview, TDC.

[287] *(SC) Greenville News*, 30 June 1935.

[288] Lester Brown, interview, TDC; Fay L. Lanford Sr., interview, TDC; Campbell and Sons, interview, TDC; Alex Campbell, interview, TDC; Pink and Ola Campbell, interview, TDC; Albert Emory, interview, TDC; Maynard Emory, interview, TDC; Lois Harrison, James W. Harrison, T.A. Hyder, interview, TDC; Alvin Howard, interview, TDC; Dr. James Howard, interview, TDC; James Hughes, interview, TDC; Fay Lanford, interview, TDC; Junior and Sylvia Pittman, interview, TDC; Ella Plumley, interview, TDC.

[289] *Greenville (SC) Mountaineer*, 19 January 1870; 20 April 1870; *Greenville (SC) Enterprise and Mountaineer,* 10 March 1887;18 April 1897;15 February 1888; 26 August 1891; *Greenville (SC) Mountaineer,* 15 February 1893; 10 April 1893; 9 August 1893; 8 November 1893; 20 November 1893; 21 February 1894; 13 June 1894; 28 November 1894; 13 April 1895; 3 July 1895;14 August 1897; 4 December 1897; 18 March 1900; 14 November 1900; 1 March 1902; 5 November 1902; 20 February 1904; 27 February 1904; *(SC) Greenville* News, 27 February 1906; *(SC) Greenville Daily* News, 13 July 1906; 14 February 1908; 19 June 1915.

[290] Pink and Ola Campbell, interview, TDC.

[291] Batson, *The Upper Part of Greenville,* 471.

[292] Thomas D. West, interview, TDC.

[293] Pink and Ola Campbell, interview, TDC.

[294] Anne McCuen. 1983. Interviewed by Dean Campbell. Greenville, SC. June 2, transcript, TDC.

[295] Campbell, interview, TDC.

[296] Kirby. *Rural Lost Worlds*, 84-85.

[297] Emery, interview, TDC.

[298] Ibid.

[299] Campbell, interview, TDC.

[300] *(SC) Greenville News*, 30 June 1935; 2 February 1959; 29 January 1974; 10 May 1983; *(SC) Greenville Piedmont,* 18 April 1989.

[301] Lawrence, *The Shadows of Hogback*, 4; Huff, *Greenville*, 14-16, 18-19, 27-28, 136, 142; *Greenville (SC) Mountaineer,* 19 November 1898.

Notes to Conclusion

[302] *(SC) Greenville Daily News*, 29 May 1894.

[303] *Spartanburg (SC) Carolina Spartan*, 3 January 1867.

[304] Fay L. Lanford Sr., interview, TDC.

[305] Miller, *Revenuers & Moonshiners*, 135; Greenville, SC, to Hon. Charles Devens, August 6, 1878. F 602745 Letters Received by the Department of South Carolina, 1871-1884 micro. NARA.; Marshal R. M. Wallace, to Hon. Charles Devens, August 7, 1878. F 602745 Letters Received by the Department of South Carolina, 1871-1884 micro. NARA.

[306] Allison, *Moonshine Memories* , 248-252; Downard. *Dictionary of the History of the American Brewing and Distilling Industries*, 238; Ellison. *Illegal Odyssey*, 135; *(SC) Spartanburg Journal*, 21 November 1974.

[307] Lou Emma Plumley, interview, TDC.

[308] Ellison, *Illegal Odyssey,* 135; Dunn, *Cades Cove*, 233.

[309] *(SC) Greenville Daily News*, 29 May 1894.

[310] *(SC) Greenville News*, 30 June 1935.

[311] Carlton, *Mill and Town,* 148-49.

[312] Charles W. Schmidt, "Sprawl: The New Manifest Destiny?," *Environmental Health Perspectives* 112 (August 2004), 622.

[313] *(SC) Greenville Piedmont*, 18 April 1989.

[314] Ibid.

[315] Hidden Hills of Glassy Mountain, "Discover the Hidden Glory," http://www.hiddenhillsofglassymtn.com/ [accessed March 27, 2008].

[316] Cliffs at Glassy, "SC country club living," http://www.cliffscommunities.com/cliffs-living/ [accessed March 19, 2008].

[317] Foothills Trail Conference, "A 76 mile woodland path along the Blue Ridge

Escarpment in northwestern South Carolina," http://www.foothillstrail.org/ [accessed March 19, 2008].

[318] Tryon Real Estate, "Rustic Mountain Living," http://www.tryon-real-estate-and-homes.com/cliffs/ [accessed March 27, 2008].

[319] For contemporary perceptions of modern Appalachian culture see Shelby Lee Adams, *Appalachian Lives* (Jackson: University of Mississippi Press, 2003); *Appalachian Legacy: Photographs* (Jackson: University of Mississippi Press, 1998); *Appalachian Portraits* (Jackson: University of Mississippi Press, 1993).

[320] Greenville Chamber of Commerce, "Quality of Life in Greenville," http://www. greenvillechamber.org [accessed March 27, 2008].

Index

www.ingramcontent.com/pod-product-compliance
Lightning Source LLC
Chambersburg PA
CBHW031321290526
45784CB00014B/594